THE PUBLIC
AND ITS PROBLEMS

BY
JOHN DEWEY

SWALLOW PRESS

ATHENS, OHIO • CHICAGO

Swallow Press Books
are published by
Ohio University Press
Athens, Ohio 45701

ISBN 0-8040-0254-1
LIBRARY OF CONGRESS CATALOG CARD NUMBER 76-178242

JOHN DEWEY
1859-1952

CONTENTS

FOREWORD

This volume is the result of lectures delivered during the month of January, nineteen hundred and twenty-six, upon the Larwill Foundation of Kenyon College, Ohio. In acknowledging the many courtesies received, I wish to express also my appreciation of the toleration shown by the authorities of the College to delay in publication. The intervening period has permitted a full revision and expansion of the lectures as originally delivered. This fact will account for an occasional reference to books published in the interval.

J. D.

THE PUBLIC
AND ITS PROBLEMS

CHAPTER I

SEARCH FOR THE PUBLIC

If one wishes to realize the distance which may lie between "facts" and the meaning of facts, let one go to the field of social discussion. Many persons seem to suppose that facts carry their meaning along with themselves on their face. Accumulate enough of them, and their interpretation stares out at you. The development of physical science is thought to confirm the idea. But the power of physical facts to coerce belief does not reside in the bare phenomena. It proceeds from method, from the technique of research and calculation. No one is ever forced by just the collection of facts to accept a particular theory of their meaning, so long as one retains intact some other doctrine by which he can marshal them. Only when the facts are allowed free play for the suggestion of new points of view is any significant conversion of conviction as to meaning possible. Take away from physical science its laboratory apparatus and its mathematical technique, and the human imagination might run wild in its theories of interpretation even if we suppose the brute facts to remain the same.

In any event, social philosophy exhibits an immense gap between facts and doctrines. Compare, for ex-

3

ample, the facts of politics with the theories which are extant regarding the nature of the state. If inquirers confine themselves to observed phenomena, the behavior of kings, presidents, legislators, judges, sheriffs, assessors and all other public officials, surely a reasonable consensus is not difficult to attain. Contrast with this agreement the differences which exist as to the basis, nature, functions and justification of the state, and note the seemingly hopeless disagreement. If one asks not for an enumeration of facts, but for a definition of the state, one is plunged into controversy, into a medley of contradictory clamors. According to one tradition, which claims to derive from Aristotle, the state is associated and harmonized life lifted to its highest potency; the state is at once the keystone of the social arch and is the arch in its wholeness. According to another view, it is just one of many social institutions, having a narrow but important function, that of arbiter in the conflict of other social units. Every group springs out of and realizes a positive human interest; the church, religious values; guilds, unions and corporations material economic interests, and so on. The state, however, has no concern of its own; its purpose is formal, like that of the leader of the orchestra who plays no instrument and makes no music, but who serves to keep other players who do produce music in unison with one another. Still a third view has it that the state is organized oppression, at once a social excrescence, a parasite and a tyrant. A fourth is that it is an instrument more or less clumsy for keeping individuals from quarreling too much with one another.

Confusion grows when we enter subdivisions of these different views and the grounds offered for them. In one philosophy, the state is the apex and completion of human association, and manifests the highest realization of all distinctively human capacities. The view had a certain pertinency when it was first formulated. It developed in an antique city-state, where to be fully a free man and to be a citizen participating in the drama, the sports, the religion and the government of the community were equivalent affairs. But the view persists and is applied to the state of to-day. Another view coördinates the state with the church (or as a variant view slightly subordinates it to the latter) as the secular arm of Deity maintaining outward order and decorum among men. A modern theory idealizes the state and its activities by borrowing the conceptions of reason and will, magnifying them till the state appears as the objectified manifestation of a will and reason which far transcend the desires and purposes which can be found among individuals or assemblages of individuals.

We are not concerned, however, with writing either a cyclopedia or history of political doctrines. So we pause with these arbitrary illustrations of the proposition that little common ground has been discovered between the factual phenomena of political behavior and the interpretation of the meaning of these phenomena. One way out of the impasse is to consign the whole matter of meaning and interpretation to political philosophy as distinguished from political science. Then it can be pointed out that futile speculation is a companion of all philosophy. The moral is to drop all doctrines of this kind overboard, and stick to facts verifiably ascertained.

The remedy urged is simple and attractive. But it is not possible to employ it. Political facts are not outside human desire and judgment. Change men's estimate of the *value* of existing political agencies and forms, and the latter change more or less. The different theories which mark political philosophy do not grow up externally to the facts which they aim to interpret; they are amplifications of selected factors among those facts. Modifiable and altering human habits sustain and generate political phenomena. These habits are not wholly informed by reasoned purpose and deliberate choice—far from it—but they are more or less amenable to them. Bodies of men are constantly engaged in attacking and trying to change some political habits, while other bodies of men are actively supporting and justifying them. It is mere pretense, then, to suppose that we can stick by the *de facto*, and not raise at some points the question of *de jure*: the question of by what right, the question of legitimacy. And such a question has a way of growing until it has become a question as to the nature of the state itself.

The alternatives before us are not factually limited science on one hand and uncontrolled speculation on the other. The choice is between blind, unreasoned attack and defense on the one hand, and discriminating criticism employing intelligent method and a conscious criterion on the other.

The prestige of the mathematical and physical sciences is great, and properly so. But the difference between facts which are what they are independent of human desire and endeavor and facts which are to some extent what they are because of human interest and purpose, and which alter with alteration in the latter, cannot be got rid of by any methodology. The more sincerely we appeal to facts, the greater is the importance of the distinction between facts which condition human activity and facts which are conditioned by human activity. In the degree which we ignore this difference, social science becomes pseudo-science. Jeffersonian and Hamiltonian political ideas are not merely theories dwelling in the human mind remote from facts of American political behavior. They are expressions of chosen phases and factors among those facts, but they are also something more: namely, forces which have shaped those facts and which are still contending to shape them in the future this way and that. There is more than a speculative difference between a theory of the state which regards it as an instrument in protecting individuals in the rights they already have, and one which conceives its function to be the effecting of a more equitable distribution of rights among individuals. For the theories are held and applied by legislators in congress and by judges on the bench and make a difference in the subsequent facts themselves.

I make no doubt that the practical influence of the political philosophies of Aristotle, the Stoics, St. Thomas, Locke, Rousseau, Kant and Hegel has often been exaggerated in comparison with the influence of circumstances. But a due measure of efficacy cannot be denied them on the ground which is sometimes proffered; it cannot be denied on the ground that ideas are without potency. For ideas belong to human beings who have bodies, and there is no separation between the structures and processes of the part of the body that entertains the ideas and the part that performs acts. Brain and muscles work together, and the brains of men are much more important data for social science than are their muscular system and their sense organs.

It is not our intention to engage in a discussion of political philosophies. The concept of the state, like most concepts which are introduced by "The," is both too rigid and too tied up with controversies to be of ready use. It is a concept which can be approached by a flank movement more easily than by a frontal attack. The moment we utter the words "The State" a score of intellectual ghosts rise to obscure our vision. Without our intention and without our notice, the notion of "The State" draws us imperceptibly into a

consideration of the logical relationship of various
ideas to one another, and away from facts of human
activity. It is better, if possible, to start from the
latter and see if we are not led thereby into an idea
of something which will turn out to implicate the marks
and signs which characterize political behavior.

There is nothing novel in this method of approach.
But very much depends upon what we select from which
to start and very much depends upon whether we select
our point of departure in order to tell at the terminus
what the state *ought* to be or what it *is*. If we are
too concerned with the former, there is a likelihood
that we shall unwittingly have doctored the facts
selected in order to come out at a predetermined point.
The phase of human action we should *not* start with
is that to which direct causative power is attributed.
We should not look for state-forming forces. If we
do, we are likely to get involved in mythology. To
explain the origin of the state by saying that man is
a political animal is to travel in a verbal circle. It
is like attributing religion to a religious instinct, the
family to marital and parental affection, and language
to a natural endowment which impels men to speech.
Such theories merely reduplicate in a so-called causal
force the effects to be accounted for. They are of a
piece with the notorious potency of opium to put men
to sleep because of its dormitive power.

The warning is not directed against a man of straw.
The attempt to derive the state, or any other social

institution, from strictly "psychological" data is in
point. Appeal to a gregarious instinct to account
for social arrangements is the outstanding example of
the lazy fallacy. Men do not run together and join
in a larger mass as do drops of quicksilver, and if
they did the result would not be a state nor any mode
of human association. The instincts, whether named
gregariousness, or sympathy, or the sense of mutual
dependence, or domination on one side and abasement
and subjection on the other, at best account for everything in general and nothing in particular. And at
worst, the alleged instinct and natural endowment appealed to as a causal force themselves represent physiological tendencies which have previously been shaped
into habits of action and expectation by means of the
very social conditions they are supposed to explain.
Men who have lived in herds develop attachment to the
horde to which they have become used; children who
have perforce lived in dependence grow into habits of
dependence and subjection. The inferiority complex is
socially acquired, and the "instinct" of display and
mastery is but its other face. There are structural
organs which physiologically manifest themselves in
vocalizations as the organs of a bird induce song. But
the barking of dogs and the song of birds are
enough to prove that these native tendencies do not
generate language. In order to be converted into language, native vocalization requires transformation by
extrinsic conditions, both organic and extra-organic or

environmental: formation, be it noted, not just stimulation. The cry of a baby can doubtless be described in purely organic terms, but the wail becomes a noun or verb only by its consequences in the responsive behavior of others. This responsive behavior takes the form of nurture and care, themselves dependent upon tradition, custom and social patterns. Why not postulate an "instinct" of infanticide as well as one of guidance and instruction? Or an "instinct" of exposing girls and taking care of boys?

We may, however, take the argument in a less mythological form than is found in the current appeal to social instincts of one sort or another. The activities of animals, like those of minerals and plants, are correlated with their structure. Quadrupeds run, worms crawl, fish swim, birds fly. They are made that way; it is "the nature of the beast." We do not gain anything by inserting instincts to run, creep, swim and fly between the structure and the act. But the strictly organic conditions which lead men to join, assemble, foregather, combine, are just those which lead other animals to unite in swarms and packs and herds. In describing what is common in human and other animal junctions and consolidations we fail to touch what is distinctively human in human associations. These structural conditions and acts may be *sine qua nons* of human societies; but so are the attractions and repulsions which are exhibited in inanimate things. Physics and chemistry as well as zoölogy may inform us of some of the conditions without which human beings would not associate. But they do not furnish us with the *sufficient* conditions of community life and of the forms which it takes.

We must in any case start from acts which are performed, not from hypothetical causes for those acts, and consider their consequences. We must also introduce intelligence, or the observation of consequences *as* consequences, that is, in connection with the acts from which they proceed. Since we must introduce it, it is better to do so knowingly than it is to smuggle it in in a way which deceives not only the customs officer—the reader—but ourselves as well. We take then our point of departure from the objective fact that human acts have consequences upon others, that some of these consequences are perceived, and that their perception leads to subsequent effort to control action so as to secure some consequences and avoid others. Following this clew, we are led to remark that the consequences are of two kinds, those which affect the persons directly engaged in a transaction, and those which affect others beyond those immediately concerned. In this distinction we find the germ of the distinction between the private and the public. When indirect consequences are recognized and there is effort to regulate them, something having the traits of a state comes into existence. When the consequences of an action are confined, or are thought to be confined, mainly to the persons directly engaged in it, the transaction is a private one. When A and B carry on a conversation together the action is a trans-action: both are concerned in it; its results pass, as it were, across from one to the other. One or other or both may be helped or harmed thereby. But, presumably, the consequences of advantage and injury do not extend beyond A and B; the activity lies between them; it is private. Yet if it is found that the consequences of conversation extend beyond the two directly concerned, that they affect the welfare of many others, the act acquires a public capacity, whether the conversation be carried on by a king and his prime minister or by Cataline and a fellow conspirator or by merchants planning to monopolize a market.

The distinction between private and public is thus in no sense equivalent to the distinction between individual and social, even if we suppose that the latter distinction has a definite meaning. Many private acts are social; their consequences contribute to the welfare of the community or affect its status and prospects. In the broad sense any transaction deliberately carried on between two or more persons is social in quality. It is a form of associated behavior and its consequences may influence further associations. A man may serve others, even in the community at large, in carrying on a private business. To some extent it is true, as Adam Smith asserted, that our breakfast table is better supplied by the convergent outcome of activities of farmers, grocers and butchers carrying

on private affairs with a view to private profit than
it would be if we were served on a basis of philanthropy
or public spirit. Communities have been supplied with
works of art, with scientific discoveries, because of the
personal delight found by private persons in engaging
in these activities. There are private philanthropists
who act so that needy persons or the community as
a whole profit by the endowment of libraries, hospitals
and educational institutions. In short, private acts
may be socially valuable both by indirect consequences
and by direct intention.

There is therefore no necessary connection between
the private character of an act and its non-social or
anti-social character. The public, moreover, cannot be
identified with the socially useful. One of the most
regular activities of the politically organized community has been waging war. Even the most bellicose
of militarists will hardly contend that all wars have
been socially helpful, or deny that some have been so
destructive of social values that it would have been
infinitely better if they had not been waged. The
argument for the non-equivalence of the public and the
social, in any praiseworthy sense of social, does not rest
upon the case of war alone. There is no one, I suppose,
so enamored of political action as to hold that it has
never been short-sighted, foolish and harmful. There
are even those who hold that the presumption is always
that social loss will result from agents of the public
doing anything which could be done by persons in their

private capacity. There are many more who protest
that some special public activity, whether prohibition,
a protective tariff or the expanded meaning given the
Monroe Doctrine, is baleful to society. Indeed every
serious political dispute turns upon the question
whether a given political act is socially beneficial or
harmful.

Just as behavior is not anti-social or non-social because privately undertaken, it is not necessarily socially
valuable because carried on in the name of the public
by public agents. The argument has not carried us
far, but at least it has warned us against identifying
the community and its interests with the state or the
politically organized community. And the differentiation may dispose us to look with more favor upon
the proposition already advanced: namely, that the
line between private and public is to be drawn on the
basis of the extent and scope of the consequences of
acts which are so important as to need control, whether
by inhibition or by promotion. We distinguish private
and public buildings, private and public schools, private paths and public highways, private assets and
public funds, private persons and public officials. It
is our thesis that in this distinction we find the key to
the nature and office of the state. It is not without significance that etymologically "private" is defined in
opposition to "official," a private person being one deprived of public position. The public consists of all
those who are affected by the indirect consequences of

transactions to such an extent that it is deemed necessary to have those consequences systematically cared for. Officials are those who look out for and take care of the interests thus affected. Since those who are indirectly affected are not direct participants in the transactions in question, it is necessary that certain persons be set apart to represent them, and see to it that their interests are conserved and protected. The buildings, property, funds, and other physical resources involved in the performance of this office are *res publica*, the common-wealth. The public as far as organized by means of officials and material agencies to care for the extensive and enduring indirect consequences of transactions between persons is the *Populus*.

It is a commonplace that legal agencies for protecting the persons and properties of members of a community, and for redressing wrongs .which they suffer, did not always exist. Legal institutions derive from an earlier period when the right of self-help obtained. If a person was harmed, it was strictly up to him what he should do to get even. Injuring another and exacting a penalty for an injury received were private transactions. They were the affairs of those directly concerned and nobody else's direct business. But the injured party obtained readily the help of friends and relatives, and the aggressor did likewise. Hence consequences of the quarrel did not remain confined to those immediately concerned. Feuds ensued, and the blood-quarrel might implicate large numbers and endure for generations. The recognition of this extensive and lasting embroilment and the harm wrought by it to whole families brought a public into existence. The transaction ceased to concern only the immediate parties to it. Those indirectly affected formed a public which took steps to conserve its interests by instituting composition and other means of pacification to localize the trouble.

The facts are simple and familiar. But they seem to present in embryonic form the traits that define a state, its agencies and officers. The instance illustrates what was meant when it said that it is fallacy to try to determine the nature of the state in terms of direct causal factors. Its essential point has to do with the enduring and extensive consequences of behavior, which like all behavior proceeds in ultimate analysis through individual human beings. Recognition of evil consequences brought about a common interest which required for its maintenance certain measures and rules, together with the selection of certain persons as their guardians, interpreters, and, if need be, their executors.

If the account given is at all in the right direction, it explains the gap already mentioned between the facts of political action and theories of the state. Men have looked in the wrong place. They have sought for the key to the nature of the state in the field of agencies, in that of doers of deeds, or in some will or purpose back of the deeds. They have sought to explain

the state in terms of authorship. Ultimately all deliberate choices proceed from somebody in particular;
acts are performed by somebody, and all arrangements
and plans are made by somebody in the most concrete
sense of "somebody." Some John Doe and Richard Roe
figure in every transaction. We shall not, then, find
the public if we look for it on the side of originators of
voluntary actions. Some John Smith and his con-
geners decide whether or not to grow wheat and how
much, where and how to invest money, what roads to
build and travel, whether to wage war and if so how,
what laws to pass and which to obey and disobey.
The actual alternative to deliberate acts of individuals
is not action by the public; it is routine, impulsive and
other unreflected acts also performed by individuals.

Individual human beings may lose their identity in
a mob or in a political convention or in a joint-stock
corporation or at the polls. But this does not mean
that some mysterious collective agency is making decisions, but that some few persons who know what they
are about are taking advantage of massed force to
conduct the mob their way, boss a political machine,
and manage the affairs of corporate business. When
the public or state is involved in making social arrangements like passing laws, enforcing a contract, confer-
ring a franchise, it still acts through concrete persons.
The persons are now officers, representatives of a public and shared interest. The difference is an important
one. But it is not a difference between single human

beings and a collective impersonal will. It is between
persons in their private and in their official or representative character. The quality presented is not
authorship but authority, the authority of recognized
consequences to control the behavior which generates
and averts extensive and enduring results of weal and
woe. Officials are indeed public agents, but agents in
the sense of factors doing the business of others in
securing and obviating consequences that concern
them.

When we look in the wrong place we naturally do
not find what we are looking for. The worst of it
is, however, that looking in the wrong place, to causal
forces instead of consequences, the outcome of the
looking becomes arbitrary. There is no check on it.
"Interpretation" runs wild. Hence the variety of conflicting theories and the lack of consensus of opinion.
One might argue *a priori* that the continual conflict of
theories about the state is itself proof that the problem
has been wrongly posed. For, as we have previously
remarked, the main facts of political action, while the
phenomena vary immensely with diversity of time and
place, are not hidden even when they are complex.
They are facts of human behavior accessible to human
observation. Existence of a multitude of contradictory theories of the state, which is so baffling from the
standpoint of the theories themselves, is readily ex-
plicable the moment we see that all the theories,
in spite of their divergence from one another, spring

from a root of shared error: the taking of causal
agency instead of consequences as the heart of the problem.

Given this attitude and postulate, some men at some
time will find the causal agency in a metaphysical nisus
attributed to nature; and the state will then be explained in terms of an "essence" of man realizing itself
in an end of perfected Society.   Others, influenced by
other preconceptions and other desires, will find the required author in the will of God reproducing through
the medium of fallen humanity such an image of divine
order and justice as the corrupt material allows.
Others seek for it in the meeting of the wills of individuals who come together and by contract or mutual
pledging of loyalties bring a state into existence.   Still
others find it in an autonomous and transcendent will
embodied in all men as a universal within their particular beings, a will which by its own inner nature commands the establishment of external conditions in which
it is possible for will to express outwardly its freedom.
Others find it in the fact that mind or reason is either an
attribute of reality or is reality itself, while they con-
dole that difference and plurality of minds, individuality, is an illusion attributable to sense, or is merely an
appearance in contrast with the monistic reality of reason.   When various opinions all spring from a common
and shared error, one is as good as another, and the
accidents of education, temperament, class interest and
the dominant circumstances of the age decide which is

adopted. Reason comes into play only to find justification for the opinion which has been adopted, instead of to analyze human behavior with respect to its consequences and to frame polities accordingly. It is an old story that natural philosophy steadily progressed only after an intellectual revolution. This consisted in abandoning the search for causes and forces and turning to the analysis of what is going on and how it goes on. Political philosophy has still in large measure to take to heart this lesson.

The failure to note that the problem is that of perceiving in a discriminating and thorough way the consequences of human action (including negligence and inaction) and of instituting measures and means of caring for these consequences is not confined to production of conflicting and irreconcilable theories of the state. The failure has also had the effect of perverting the views of those who, up to a certain point, perceived the truth. We have asserted that all deliberate choices and plans are finally the work of single human beings. Thoroughly false conclusions have been drawn from this observation. By thinking still in terms of causal forces, the conclusion has been drawn from this fact that the state, the public, is a fiction, a mask for private desires for power and position. Not only the state but society itself has been pulverized into an aggregate of unrelated wants and wills. As a logical consequence, the state is conceived either as sheer oppression born of arbitrary power and sustained in fraud, or as a pooling of the forces of single men into a massive force which single persons are unable to resist, the pooling being a measure of desperation since its sole alternative is the conflict of all with all which generates a life that is helpless and brutish. Thus the state appears either a monster to be destroyed or as a Leviathan to be cherished. In short, under the influence of the prime fallacy that the problem of the state concerns causal forces, individualism, as an ism, as a philosophy, has been generated.

While the doctrine is false, it sets out from a fact. Wants, choices and purposes have their locus in single beings; behavior which manifests desire, intent and resolution proceeds from them in their singularity. But only intellectual laziness leads us to conclude that since the form of thought and decision is individual, their content, their subject-matter, is also something purely personal. Even if "consciousness" were the wholly private matter that the individualistic tradition in philosophy and psychology supposes it to be, it would still be true that consciousness is *of* objects, not of itself. Association in the sense of connection and combination is a "law" of everything known to exist. Singular things act, but they act together. Nothing has been discovered which acts in entire isolation. The action of everything is along with the action of other things. The "along with" is of such a kind that the behavior of each is modified by its connection with others. There are trees which can grow only in a forest. Seeds

of many plants can successfully germinate and develop
only under conditions furnished by the presence of
other plants. Reproduction of kind is dependent upon
the activities of insects which bring about fertilization.
The life-history of an animal cell is conditioned upon
connection with what other cells are doing. Electrons, atoms and molecules exemplify the omnipresence
of conjoint behavior.

There is no mystery about the fact of association,
of an interconnected action which affects the activity of
singular elements. There is no sense in asking how
individuals come to be associated. They exist and operate in association. If there is any mystery about the
matter, it is the mystery that the universe is the kind
of universe it is. Such a mystery could not be explained without going outside the universe. And if one
should go to an outside source to account for it, some
logician, without an excessive draft upon his ingenuity,
would rise to remark that the outsider would have to be
connected with the universe in order to account for
anything in it. We should still be just where we
started, with the fact of connection as a fact to be
accepted.

There is, however, an intelligible question about human association:—Not the question how individuals or
singular beings come to be connected, but how they
come to be connected in just those ways which give
human communities traits so different from those which
mark assemblies of electrons, unions of trees in forests,

swarms of insects, herds of sheep, and constellations of stars. When we consider the difference we at once come upon the fact that the consequences of conjoint action take on a new value when they are observed. For notice of the effects of connected action forces men to reflect upon the connection itself; it makes it an object of attention and interest. Each acts, in so far as the connection is known, in view of the connection. Individuals still do the thinking, desiring and purposing, but *what* they think of is the consequences of their behavior upon that of others and that of others upon themselves.

Each human being is born an infant. He is immature, helpless, dependent upon the activities of others. That many of these dependent beings survive is proof that others in some measure look out for them, take care of them. Mature and better equipped beings are aware of the consequences of their acts upon those of the young. They not only act conjointly with them, but they act in that especial kind of association which manifests interest in the consequences of their conduct upon the life and growth of the young.

Continued physiological existence of the young is only one phase of interest in the consequences of association. Adults are equally concerned to act so that the immature learn to think, feel, desire and habitually conduct themselves in certain ways. Not the least of the consequences which are striven for is that the young shall themselves learn to judge, purpose and

choose from the standpoint of associated behavior and
its consequences. In fact, only too often this interest
takes the form of endeavoring to make the young be-
lieve and plan just as adults do. This instance alone
is enough to show that while singular beings in their
singularity think, want and decide, *what* they think
and strive for, the content of their beliefs and intentions is a subject-matter provided by association.
Thus man is not merely *de facto* associated, but he
becomes a social animal in the make-up of his
ideas, sentiments and deliberate behavior. *What* he
believes, hopes for and aims at is the outcome of association and intercourse. The only thing which imports
obscurity and mystery into the influence of association
upon what individual persons want and act for is the
effort to discover alleged, special, original, society-mak-
ing causal forces, whether instincts, fiats of will, personal, or an immanent, universal, practical reason, or
an indwelling, metaphysical, social essence and nature.
These things do not explain, for they are more mysterious than are the facts they are evoked to account
for. The planets in a constellation would form a community if they were aware of the connections of the
activities of each with those of the others and could
use this knowledge to direct behavior.

We have made a digression from consideration of
the state to the wider topic of society. However, the
excursion enables us to distinguish the state from other
forms of social life. There is an old tradition which

regards the state and completely organized society as the same thing. The state is said to be the complete and inclusive realization of all social institutions. Whatever values result from any and every social arrangement are gathered together and asserted to be the work of the state. The counterpart of this method is that philosophical anarchism which assembles all the evils that result from all forms of human grouping and attributes them *en masse* to the state, whose elimination would then bring in a millennium of voluntary fraternal organization. That the state should be to some a deity and to others a devil is another evidence of the defects of the premises from which discussion sets out. One theory is as indiscriminate as the other.

There is, however, a definite criterion by which to demarcate the organized public from other modes of community life. Friendships, for example, are non-political forms of association. They are characterized by an intimate and subtle sense of the fruits of intercourse. They contribute to experience some of its most precious values. Only the exigencies of a preconceived theory would confuse with the state that texture of friendships and attachments which is the chief bond in any community, or would insist that the former depends upon the latter for existence. Men group themselves also for scientific inquiry, for religious worship, for artistic production and enjoyment, for sport, for giving and receiving instruction, for industrial and commercial undertakings. In each case some combined or conjoint action, which has grown up out of "natural," that is, biological, conditions and from local contiguity, results in producing distinctive consequences—that is, consequences which differ in kind from those of isolated behavior.

When these consequences are intellectually and emotionally appreciated, a shared interest is generated and the nature of the interconnected behavior is thereby transformed. Each form of association has its own peculiar quality and value, and no person in his senses confuses one with another. The characteristic of the public as a state springs from the fact that all modes of associated behavior may have extensive and enduring consequences which involve others beyond those directly engaged in them. When these consequences are in turn realized in thought and sentiment, recognition of them reacts to remake the conditions out of which they arose. Consequences have to be taken care of, looked out for. This supervision and regulation cannot be effected by the primary groupings themselves. For the essence of the consequences which call a public into being is the fact that they expand beyond those directly engaged in producing them. Consequently special agencies and measures must be formed if they are to be attended to; or else some existing group must take on new functions. The obvious external mark of the organization of a public or of a state is thus the existence of officials. Government is not the state, for that includes the public as well as the rulers charged with special duties and powers. The public, however, is organized in and through those officers who act in behalf of its interests.

Thus the state represents an important although distinctive and restricted social interest. From this point of view there is nothing extraordinary in the preëminence of the claims of the organized public over other interests when once they are called into play, nor in its total indifference and irrelevancy to friendships, associations for science, art and religion under most circumstances. If the consequences of a friendship threaten the public, then it is treated as a conspiracy; usually it is not the state's business or concern. Men join each other in partnership as a matter of course to do a piece of work more profitably or for mutual defense. Let its operations exceed a certain limit, and others not participating in it find their security or prosperity menaced by it, and suddenly the gears of the state are in mesh. Thus it happens that the state, instead of being all absorbing and inclusive, is under some circumstances the most idle and empty of social arrangements. Nevertheless, the temptation to generalize from these instances and conclude that the state generically is of no significance is at once challenged by the fact that when a family connection, a church, a trade union, a business corporation, or an educational institution conducts itself so as to affect large numbers outside of itself, those who are affected form a public which endeavors to act through suitable structures, and thus to organize itself for oversight and regulation.

I know of no better way in which to apprehend the absurdity of the claims which are sometimes made in behalf of society politically organized than to call to mind the influence upon community life of Socrates, Buddha, Jesus, Aristotle, Confucius, Homer, Vergil, Dante, St. Thomas, Shakespeare, Copernicus, Galileo, Newton, Boyle, Locke, Rousseau and countless others, and then to ask ourselves if we conceive these men to be officers of the state. Any method which so broadens the scope of the state as to lead to such conclusion merely makes the state a name for the totality of all kinds of associations. The moment we have taken the word as loosely as that, it is at once necessary to distinguish, within it, the state in its usual political and legal sense. On the other hand, if one is tempted to eliminate or disregard the state, one may think of Pericles, Alexander, Julius and Augustus Cæsar, Elizabeth, Cromwell, Richelieu, Napoleon, Bismarck and hundreds of names of that kind. One dimly feels that they must have had a private life, but how insignificant it bulks in comparison with their action as representatives of a state!

This conception of statehood does not imply any belief as to the propriety or reasonableness of any particular political act, measure or system. Observations of consequences are at least as subject to error and illusion as is perception of natural objects. Judgments about what to undertake so as to regulate them, and how to do it, are as fallible as other plans. Mistakes pile up and consolidate themselves into laws and methods of administration which are more harmful than the consequences which they were originally intended to control. And as all political history shows, the power and prestige which attend command of official position render rule something to be grasped and exploited for its own sake. Power to govern is distributed by the accident of birth or by the possession of qualities which enable a person to obtain office, but which are quite irrelevant to the performance of its representative functions. But the need which calls forth the organization of the public by means of rulers and agencies of government persists and to some extent is incarnated in political fact. Such progress as political history records depends upon some luminous emergence of the idea from the mass of irrelevancies which obscure and clutter it. Then some reconstruction occurs which provides the function with organs more apt for its fulfillment. Progress is not steady and continuous. Retrogression is as periodic as advance. Industry and inventions in technology, for example, create means which alter the modes of associated behavior and which radically change the quantity, character and place of impact of their indirect consequences.

These changes are extrinsic to political forms which, once established, persist of their own momentum. The

new public which is generated remains long inchoate, unorganized, because it cannot use inherited political agencies. The latter, if elaborate and well institutionalized, obstruct the organization of the new public.
They prevent that development of new forms of the
state which might grow up rapidly were social life more
fluid, less precipitated into set political and legal
molds. To form itself, the public has to break existing
political forms. This is hard to do because these forms
are themselves the regular means of instituting change.
The public which generated political forms is passing
away, but the power and lust of possession remains in
the hands of the officers and agencies which the dying
public instituted. This is why the change of the form
of states is so often effected only by revolution. The
creation of adequately flexible and responsive political
and legal machinery has so far been beyond the wit of
man. An epoch in which the needs of a newly forming
public are counteracted by established forms of the
state is one in which there is increasing disparagement and disregard of the state. General apathy, neglect and contempt find expression in resort to various
short-cuts of direct action. And direct action is taken
by many other interests than those which employ "direct
action" as a slogan, often most energetically by in-
trenched class-interests which profess the greatest reverence for the established "law and order" of the existing state. By its very nature, a state is ever something to be scrutinized, investigated, searched for. Al-

most as soon as its form is stabilized, it needs to be re-made.

Thus the problem of discovering the state is not a problem for theoretical inquirers engaged solely in surveying institutions which already exist. It is a practical problem of human beings living in association with one another, of mankind generically. It is a complex problem. It demands power to perceive and recognize the consequences of the behavior of individuals joined in groups and to trace them to their source and origin. It involves selection of persons to serve as representatives of the interests created by these perceived consequences and to define the functions which they shall possess and employ. It requires institution of a government such that those having the renown and power which goes with the exercise of these functions shall employ them for the public and not turn them to their own private benefit. It is no cause for wonder, then, that states have been many, not only in number but in type and kind. For there have been countless forms of joint activity with correspondingly diverse consequences. Power to detect consequences has varied especially with the instrumentalities of knowledge at hand. Rulers have been selected on all kinds of different grounds. Their functions have varied and so have their will and zeal to represent common interests. Only the exigencies of a rigid philosophy can lead us to suppose that there is some one form or idea of The State which these protean historic states have realized in

various degrees of perfection. The only statement
which can be made is a purely formal one: the state is
the organization of the public effected through officials
for the protection of the interests shared by its members. But what the public may be, what the officials
are, how adequately they perform their function, are
things we have to go to history to discover.

Nevertheless, our conception gives a criterion for determining how good a particular state is: namely, the
degree of organization of the public which is attained,
and the degree in which its officers are so constituted as
to perform their function of caring for public interests.
But there is no *a priori* rule which can be laid down and
by which when it is followed a good state will be brought
into existence. In no two ages or places is there the
same public. Conditions make the consequences of
associated action and the knowledge of them different.
In addition the means by which a public can determine
the government to serve its interests vary. Only formally can we say what the best state would be. In concrete fact, in actual and concrete organization and
structure, there is no form of state which can be said to
be the best: not at least till history is ended, and one can
survey all its varied forms. The formation of states
must be an experimental process. The trial process
may go on with diverse degrees of blindness and accident, and at the cost of unregulated procedures of cut
and try, of fumbling and groping, without insight into
what men are after or clear knowledge of a good state

even when it is achieved. Or it may proceed more intelligently, because guided by knowledge of the conditions which must be fulfilled. But it is still experimental. And since conditions of action and of inquiry
and knowledge are always changing, the experiment
must always be retried; the State must always be redis-
covered. Except, once more, in formal statement of
conditions to be met, we have no idea what history may
still bring forth. It is not the business of political
philosophy and science to determine what the state in
general should or must be. What they may do is to aid
in creation of methods such that experimentation may
go on less blindly, less at the mercy of accident, more
intelligently, so that men may learn from their errors
and profit by their successes. The belief in political
fixity, of the sanctity of some form of state conse-
crated by the efforts of our fathers and hallowed by
tradition, is one of the stumbling-blocks in the way of
orderly and directed change; it is an invitation to revolt and revolution.

As the argument has moved to and fro, it will conduce to clearness to summarize its steps. Conjoint,
combined, associated action is a universal trait of the
behavior of things. Such action has results. Some of
the results of human collective action are perceived,
that is, they are noted in such ways that they are
taken account of. Then there arise purposes, plans,
measures and means, to secure consequences which are
liked and eliminate those which are found obnoxious.
Thus perception generates a common interest; that is,

those affected by the consequences are perforce concerned in conduct of all those who along with themselves share in bringing about the results. Sometimes the consequences are confined to those who directly share in the transaction which produces them. In other cases they extend far beyond those immediately engaged in producing them. Thus two kinds of interests and of measures of regulation of acts in view of consequences are generated. In the first, interest and control are limited to those directly engaged; in the second, they extend to those who do not directly share in the performance of acts. If, then, the interest constituted by their being affected by the actions in question is to have any practical influence, control over the actions which produce them must occur by some indirect means.

So far the statements, it is submitted, set forth matters of actual and ascertainable fact. Now follows the hypothesis. Those indirectly and seriously affected for good or for evil form a group distinctive enough to require recognition and a name. The name selected is The Public. This public is organized and made effective by means of representatives who as guardians of custom, as legislators, as executives, judges, etc., care for its especial interests by methods intended to regulate the conjoint actions of individuals and groups. Then and in so far, association adds to itself political organization, and something which may be government comes into being: the public is a political state.

The direct confirmation of the hypothesis is found

in the statement of the series of observable and veri-
fiable matters of fact. These constitute conditions
which are sufficient to account, so it is held, for the
characteristic phenomena of political life, or state
activity. If they do, it is superfluous to seek for other
explanation. In conclusion, two qualifications should
be added. The account just given is meant to be
generic; it is consequently schematic, and omits many
differential conditions, some of which receive attention in subsequent chapters. The other point is that in
the negative part of the argument, the attack upon
theories which would explain the state by means of
special causal forces and agencies, there is no denial
of causal relations or connections among phenomena
themselves. That is obviously assumed at every point.
There can be no consequences and measures to regulate
the mode and quality of their occurrence without the
causal nexus. What is denied is an appeal to *special*
forces outside the series of observable connected
phenomena. Such causal powers are no different in
kind to the occult forces from which physical science
had to emancipate itself. At best, they are but phases
of the related phenomena themselves which are then
employed to account for the facts. What is needed to
direct and make fruitful social inquiry is a method
which proceeds on the basis of the interrelations of
observable acts and their results. Such is the gist of
the method we propose to follow.

CHAPTER II

DISCOVERY OF THE STATE

If we look in the wrong place for the public we shall never locate the state. If we do not ask what are the conditions which promote and obstruct the organization of the public into a social group with definite functions, we shall never grasp the problem involved in the development and transformation of states. If we do not perceive that this organization is equivalent to the equipment of the public with official representatives to care for the interests of the public, we shall miss the clew to the nature of government. These are conclusions reached or suggested by the discussion of the last hour. The wrong place to look, as we saw, is in the realm of alleged causal agency, of authorship, of forces which are supposed to produce a state by an intrinsic *vis genetrix.* The state is not created as a direct result of organic contacts as offspring are conceived in the womb, nor by direct conscious intent as a machine is invented, nor by some brooding indwelling spirit, whether a personal deity or a metaphysical absolute will. When we seek for the origin of states in such sources as these, a realistic regard for facts compels us to conclude in the end that we find nothing but singular persons, you, they, me. We shall then be

driven, unless we have recourse to mysticism, to decide
that the public is born in a myth and is sustained by
superstition.

There are many answers to the question: What is
the public? Unfortunately many of them are only
restatements of the question. Thus we are told that
the public is the community as a whole, and a-com-
munity-as-a-whole is supposed to be a self-evident and
self-explanatory phenomenon. But a community as
a *whole* involves not merely a variety of associative ties
which hold persons together in diverse ways, but an
organization of all elements by an integrated principle.
And this is precisely what we are in search of. Why
should there be anything of the nature of an all-inclusive
and regulative unity? If we postulate such a thing,
surely the institution which alone would answer to it
is humanity, not the affairs which history exhibits as
states. The notion of an inherent universality in the
associative force at once breaks against the obvious
fact of a plurality of states, each localized, with its
boundaries, limitations, its indifference and even hostility to other states. The best that metaphysical
monistic philosophies of politics can do with this fact
is to ignore it. Or, as in the case of Hegel and his
followers, a mythical philosophy of history is constructed to eke out the deficiencies of a mythical doctrine of statehood. The universal spirit seizes upon
one temporal and local nation after another as the
vehicle for its objectification of reason and will.

Such considerations as these reinforce our proposition that the perception of consequences which are projected in important ways beyond the persons and associations directly concerned in them is the source of a public; and that its organization into a state is effected by establishing special agencies to care for and regulate these consequences. But they also suggest that actual states exhibit traits which perform the function that has been stated and which serve as marks of anything to be called a state. Discussion of these traits will define the nature of the public and the problem of its political organization, and will also operate to test our theory.

We can hardly select a better trait to serve as a mark and sign of the nature of a state than a point just mentioned, temporal and geographical localization. There are associations which are too narrow and restricted in scope to give rise to a public, just as there are associations too isolated from one another to fall within the same public. Part of the problem of discovery of a public capable of organization into a state is that of drawing lines between the too close and intimate and the too remote and disconnected. Immediate contiguity, face to face relationships, have consequences which generate a community of interests, a sharing of values, too direct and vital to occasion a need for political organization. Connections within a family are familiar; they are matters of immediate acquaintance and concern. The so-called blood-tie

which has played such a part in demarcation of social
units is largely imputed on the basis of sharing immediately in the results of conjoint behavior. What
one does in the household affects others directly and
the consequences are appreciated at once and in an
intimate way. As we say, they "come home." Special
organization to care for them is a superfluity. Only
when the tie has extended to a union of families in a
clan and of clans in a tribe do consequences become
so indirect that special measures are called for. The
neighborhood is constituted largely on the same pattern
of association that is exemplified in the family.
Custom and measures improvised to meet special
emergencies as they arise suffice for its regulation.

Consider the village in Wiltshire so beautifully
described by Hudson: "Each house has its center of
human life with life of bird and beast, and the centers
were in touch with one another, connected like a row
of children linked together by their hands; all together
forming one organism, instinct with one life, moved by
one mind, like a many-colored serpent lying at rest,
extended at full length upon the ground. I imagined
the case of a cottager at one end of the village occupied in chopping up a tough piece of wood or stump
and accidentally letting fall his heavy sharp axe on to
his foot, inflicting a grievous wound. The tidings of
the accident would fly from mouth to mouth to the
other extremity of the village, a mile distant; not only
would each villager quickly know of it, but have at

the same time a vivid mental image of his fellow
villager at the moment of his misadventure, the sharp
glittering axe falling on to his foot, the red blood flowing from the wound; and he would at the same time feel
the wound in his own foot and the shock to his system.
In like manner all thoughts and feelings would pass
freely from one to another, though not necessarily
communicated by speech; and all would be participants
in virtue of that sympathy and solidarity uniting the
members of a small isolated community. No one would
be capable of a thought or emotion which would seem
strange to the others. The temper, the mood, the outlook of the individual and the village, would be the
same." [1] With such a condition of intimacy, the state
is an impertinence.

For long periods of human history, especially in
the Orient, the state is hardly more than a shadow
thrown upon the family and neighborhood by remote
personages, swollen to gigantic form by religious beliefs. It rules but it does not regulate; for its rule is
confined to receipt of tribute and ceremonial deference.
Duties are within the family; property is possessed
by the family. Personal loyalties to elders take the
place of political obedience. The relationships of husband and wife, parent and children, older and younger
children, friend and friend, are the bonds from which
authority proceeds. Politics is not a branch of morals;

[1] W. H. Hudson, "A Traveller in Little Things," pp. 110-112.

it is submerged in morals.   All virtues are summed
up in filial piety.   Wrongdoing is culpable because
it reflects upon one's ancestry and kin.   Officials are
known but only to be shunned.   To submit a dispute
to them is a disgrace.   The measure of value of the
remote and theocratic state lies in what it does *not*
do.   Its perfection is found in its identification with
the processes of nature, in virtue of which the seasons
travel their constant round, so that fields under the
beneficent rule of sun and rain produce their harvest,
and the neighborhood prospers in peace.   The intimate
and familiar propinquity group is not a social unity
within an inclusive whole.   It is, for almost all purposes, society itself.

At the other limit there are social groups so
separated by rivers, seas and mountains, by strange
languages and gods, that what one of them does—save
in war—has no appreciable consequences for another.
There is therefore no common interest, no public, and
no need nor possibility of an inclusive state.   The
plurality of states is such a universal and notorious
phenomenon that it is taken for granted.   It does not
seem to require explanation.   But it sets up, as we
have noted, a test difficult for some theories to meet.
Except upon the basis of a freakish limitation in the
common will and reason which is alleged to be the
foundation of the state, the difficulty is insuperable.   It
is peculiar, to say the least, that universal reason
should be unable to cross a mountain range and ob-

jective will be balked by a river current. The difficulty
is not so great for many other theories. But only
the theory which makes recognition of consequences
the critical factor can find in the fact of many
states a corroborating trait. Whatever is a barrier
to the spread of the consequences of associated behavior by that very fact operates to set up political
boundaries. The explanation is as commonplace as is
the thing to be explained.

Somewhere between associations that are narrow,
close and intimate and those which are so remote as
to have only infrequent and casual contact lies, then,
the province of a state. We do not find and should
not expect to find sharp and fast demarcations. Vil-
lages and neighborhoods shade imperceptibly into a
political public. Different states may pass through
federations and alliances into a larger whole which has
some of the marks of statehood. This condition, which
we should anticipate in virtue of the theory, is confirmed by historical facts. The wavering and shifting
line of distinction between a state and other forms of
social union is, again, an obstacle in the way of
theories of the state which imply as their concrete
counterpart something as sharply marked off as is
the concept. On the basis of empirical consequences,
it is just the sort of thing which should occur. There
are empires due to conquest where political rule exists
only in forced levies of taxes and soldiers, and in
which, though the word state may be used, the charac-

teristic signs of a public are notable for their absence. There are political communities like the city-states of ancient Greece in which the fiction of common descent is a vital factor, in which household gods and worship are replaced by community divinities, shrines, and cults: states in which much of the intimacy of the vivid and prompt personal touch of the family endures, while there has been added the transforming inspiration of a varied, freer, fuller life, whose issues are so momentous that in comparison the life of the neighborhood is parochial and that of the household dull.

Multiplicity and constant transformation in the forms which the state assumes are as comprehensible upon the hypothesis proposed as is the numerical diversity of independent states. The consequences of conjoint behavior differ in kind and in range with changes in "material culture," especially those involved in exchange of raw materials, finished products and above all in technology, in tools, weapons and utensils. These in turn are immediately affected by inventions in means of transit, transportation and intercommunication. A people that lives by tending flocks of sheep and cattle adapts itself to very different conditions than those of a people which ranges freely, mounted on horses. One form of nomadism is usually peaceful; the other warlike. Roughly speaking, tools and implements determine occupations, and occupations determine the consequences of associated activity. In determining consequences, they institute publics with

different interests, which exact different types of
political behavior to care for them.

In spite of the fact that diversity of political forms
rather than uniformity is the rule, belief in *the* state
as an archetypal entity persists in political philosophy
and science. Much dialectical ingenuity has been expended in construction of an essence or intrinsic nature
in virtue of which any particular association is entitled to have applied to it the concept of statehood.
Equal ingenuity has been expended in explaining away
all divergencies from this morphological type, and (the
favored device) in ranking states in a hierarchical
order of value as they approach the defining essence.
The idea that there is a model pattern which makes a
state a *good* or true state has affected practice as well
as theory. It, more than anything else, is responsible
for the effort to form constitutions offhand and impose
them ready-made on peoples. Unfortunately, when the
falsity of this view was perceived, it was replaced by
the idea that states "grow" or develop instead of being
made. This "growth" did not mean simply that states
alter. Growth signified an evolution through regular
stages to a predetermined end because of some intrinsic
nisus or principle. This theory discouraged recourse to
the only method by which alterations of political forms
might be directed: namely, the use of intelligence to
judge consequences. Equally with the theory which
it displaced, it presumed the existence of a single
standard form which defines *the* state as the essential

and true article. After a false analogy with physical
science, it was asserted that only the assumption of
such a uniformity of process renders a "scientific"
treatment of society possible. Incidentally, the theory
flattered the conceit of those nations which, being
politically "advanced," assumed that they were so near
the apex of evolution as to wear the crown of statehood.

The hypothesis presented makes possible a consistently empirical or *historical* treatment of the
changes in political forms and arrangements, free from
any overriding conceptual domination such as is inevitable when a "true" state is postulated, whether
that be thought of as deliberately made or as
evolving by its own inner law. Intrusions from non-
political internal occurrences, industrial and technological, and from external events, borrowings, travel,
migrations, explorations, wars, modify the consequences
of preëxisting associations to such an extent that new
agencies and functions are necessitated. Political
forms are also subject to alterations of a more indirect sort. Developments of better methods of thinking bring about observation of consequences which were
concealed from a vision which used coarser intellectual
tools. Quickened intellectual insight also makes possible invention of new political devices. Science has
not indeed played a large rôle. But intuitions of
statesmen and of political theorists have occasionally
penetrated into the operations of social forces in such
a way that a new turn has been given to legislation

and to administration. There is a margin of toleration in the body politic as well as in an organic body. Measures not in any sense inevitable are accommodated to after they have once been taken; and a further diversity is thereby introduced in political manners.

In short, the hypothesis which holds that publics are constituted by recognition of extensive and enduring indirect consequences of acts accounts for the relativity of states, while the theories which define them in terms of specific causal authorship imply an absoluteness which is contradicted by facts. The attempt to find by the "comparative method" structures which are common to antique and modern, to occidental and oriental states, has involved a great waste of industry. The only constant is the function of caring for and regulating the interests which accrue as the result of the complex indirect expansion and radiation of conjoint behavior.

We conclude, then, that temporal and local diversification is a prime mark of political organization, and one which, when it is analyzed, supplies a confirming test of our theory. A second mark and evidence is found in an otherwise inexplicable fact that the quantitative scope of results of conjoint behavior generates a public with need for organization. As we already noted, what are now crimes subject to public cognizance and adjudication were once private ebullitions, having the status now possessed by an insult proffered by one to another. An interesting phase of the transition from

the relatively private to the public, at least from a
limited public to a larger one, is seen in the development in England of the King's Peace. Justice until
the twelfth century was administered mainly by feudal
and shire courts, courts of hundreds, etc. Any lord
who had a sufficient number of subjects and tenants
decided controversies and imposed penalties. The
court and justice of the king was but one among many,
and primarily concerned with royalty's tenants, servants, properties and dignities. The monarchs wished,
however, to increase their revenues and expand their
power and prestige. Various devices were invented and
fictions set up by means of which the jurisdiction of
kingly courts was extended. The method was to al-
lege that various offenses, formerly attended to by
local courts, were infractions of the king's peace. The
centralizing movement went on till the king's justice
had a monopoly. The instance is significant. A
measure instigated by desire to increase the power and
profit of the royal dynasty became an impersonal
public function by bare extension. The same sort of
thing has repeatedly occurred when personal preroga-
tives have passed into normal political processes.
Something of the same sort is manifested in contemporary life when modes of private business become
"affected with a public interest" because of quantitative
expansion.

A converse instance is presented in transfer from
public to private domain of religious rites and beliefs.

As long as the prevailing mentality thought that the consequences of piety and irreligion affected the entire community, religion was of necessity a public affair. Scrupulous adherence to the customary cult was of the highest political import. Gods were tribal ancestors or founders of the community. They granted communal prosperity when they were duly acknowledged and were the authors of famine, pestilence and defeat in war if their interests were not zealously attended to. Naturally when religious acts had such extended consequences, temples were public buildings, like the agora and forum; rites were civic functions and priests public officials. Long after theocracy vanished, theurgy was a political institution. Even when disbelief was rife, few there were who would run the risk of neglecting the ceremonials.

The revolution by which piety and worship were relegated to the private sphere is often attributed to the rise of personal conscience and assertion of its rights. But this rise is just the thing to be accounted for. The supposition that it was there all the time in a submerged condition and finally dared to show itself reverses the order of events. Social changes, both intellectual and in the internal composition and external relations of peoples, took place so that men no longer connected attitudes of reverence or disrespect to the gods with the weal and woe of the community. Faith and unbelief still had serious consequences, but these were now thought to be confined to the temporal

and eternal happiness of the persons directly concerned. Given the other belief, and persecution and in-
tolerance are as justifiable as is organized hostility to
any crime; impiety is the most dangerous of all threats
to public peace and well-being. But social changes
gradually effected as one of the new functions of the
life of the community the rights of private conscience
and creed.

In general, behavior in intellectual matters has
moved from the public to the private realm. This
radical change was, of course, urged and justified on
the ground of intrinsic and sacred private right. But,
as in the special case of religious beliefs, it is strange,
if this reason be accepted, that mankind lived so long
in total unawareness of the existence of the right. In
fact, the idea of a purely private area of consciousness,
where whatever goes on has no external consequences,
was in the first instance a product of institutional
change, political and ecclesiastic, although, like other
beliefs, once it was established it had political results.
The observation that the interests of the community
are better cared for when there is permitted a large
measure of personal judgment and choice in the formation of intellectual conclusions, is an observation which
could hardly have been made until social mobility and
heterogeneity had brought about initiation and invention in technological matters and industry, and until
secular pursuits had become formidable rivals to church
and state. Even yet, however, toleration in matters of

judgment and belief is largely a negative matter. We
agree to leave one another alone (within limits) more
from recognition of evil consequences which have resulted from the opposite course rather than from any
profound belief in its positive social beneficence. As
long as the latter consequence is not widely perceived,
the so-called natural right to private judgment will remain a somewhat precarious rationalization of the
moderate amount of toleration which has come into
being. Such phenomena as the Ku Klux and legislative activity to regulate science show that the belief in liberty of thought is still superficial.

If I make an appointment with a dentist or doctor,
the transaction is primarily between us. It is my
health which is affected and his pocket-book, skill and
reputation. But exercise of the professions has consequences so wide-spread that the examination and
licensing of persons who practice them becomes a public matter. John Smith buys or sells real estate. The
transaction is effected by himself and some other person. Land, however, is of prime importance to society,
and the private transaction is hedged about with legal
regulations; evidence of transfer and ownership has to
be recorded with a public official in forms publicly
prescribed. The choice of a mate and the act of sexual
union are intimately personal. But the act is the
condition of bearing of offspring who are the means of
the perpetuation of the community. The public interest is manifested in formalities which are necessary

to make a union legal and for its legal termination. Consequences, in a word, affect large numbers beyond those immediately concerned in the transaction. It is often thought that in a socialistic state the formation and dissolution of marriages would cease to have a public phase. It is possible. But it is also possible that such a state would be even more alive than is the community at present to the consequences of the union of man and woman not only upon children but upon its own well-being and stability. In that case certain regulations would be relaxed, but there might be imposed stringent rules as to health, economic capacity and psychologic compatibility as preconditions of wedlock.

No one can take into account all the consequences of the acts he performs. It is a matter of necessity for him, as a rule, to limit his attention and foresight to matters which, as we say, are distinctively his own business. Any one who looked too far abroad with regard to the outcome of what he is proposing to do would, if there were no general rules in existence, soon be lost in a hopelessly complicated muddle of considerations. The man of most generous outlook has to draw the line somewhere, and he is forced to draw it in whatever concerns those closely associated with himself. In the absence of some objective regulation, effects upon them are all he can be sure of in any reasonable degree. Much of what is called selfishness is but the outcome of limitation of observation and

imagination. Hence when consequences concern a large
number, a number so mediately involved that a person
cannot readily prefigure how they are to be affected,
that number is constituted a public which intervenes.
It is not merely that the combined observations of a
number cover more ground than those of a single
person. It is rather that the public itself, being unable
to forecast and estimate all consequences, establishes
certain dikes and channels so that actions are confined
within prescribed limits, and insofar have moderately
predictable consequences.

The regulations and laws of the state are therefore
misconceived when they are viewed as commands. The
"command" theory of common and statute law is in
reality a dialectical consequence of the theories, previously criticized, which define the state in terms of an
antecedent causation, specifically of that theory which
takes "will" to be the causal force which generates the
state. If a will is the origin of the state, then state-ac-
tion expresses itself in injunctions and prohibitions
imposed by its will upon the wills of subjects. Sooner
or later, however, the question arises as to the justification of the will which issues commands. Why should
the will of the rulers have more authority than that of
others? Why should the latter submit? The logical
conclusion is that the ground of obedience lies ultimately in superior force. But this conclusion is an
obvious invitation to trial of forces to see where superior force lies. In fact the idea of authority is abol-

ished, and that of force substituted. The next dialectical conclusion is that the will in question is something
over and above any private will or any collection of
such wills: is some overruling "general will." This
conclusion was drawn by Rousseau, and under the influence of German metaphysics was erected into a
dogma of a mystic and transcendent absolute will,
which in turn was not another name for force only
because it was identified with absolute reason. The
alternative to one or other of these conclusions is surrender of the causal authorship theory and the adoption of that of widely distributed consequences, which,
when they are perceived, create a common interest and
the need of special agencies to care for it.

Rules of law are in fact the institution of conditions
under which persons make their arrangements with one
another. They are structures which canalize action;
they are active forces only as are banks which confine
the flow of a stream, and are commands only in the
sense in which the banks command the current. If individuals had no stated conditions under which they
come to agreement with one another, any agreement
would either terminate in a twilight zone of vagueness
or would have to cover such an enormous amount of
detail as to be unwieldy and unworkable. Each agreement, moreover, might vary so from every other that
nothing could be inferred from one arrangement as to
the probable consequences of any other. Legal rules
state certain conditions which when met make an agree-

ment a contract. The terms of the agreement are
thereby canalized within manageable limits, and it is
possible to generalize and predict from one to another.
Only the exigencies of a theory lead one to hold that
there is a command that an agreement be made in such
and such a form.[2] What happens is that certain conditions are set such that *if* a person conform to them,
he can count on certain consequences, while if he fails
to do so he cannot forecast consequences. He takes a
chance and runs the risk of having the whole transaction invalidated to his loss. There is no reason to interpret even the "prohibitions" of criminal law in any
other way. Conditions are stated in reference to consequences which may be incurred if they are infringed
or transgressed. We can similarly state the undesirable results which will happen if a stream breaks
through its banks; if the stream were capable of foreseeing these consequences and directing its behaviour by
the foresight, we might metaphorically construe the
banks as issuing a prohibition.

This account explains both the large arbitrary and
contingent element in laws and their plausible identification with reason, dissimilar as are the two considerations. There are many transactions in which the thing
of chief importance is that consequences be determinate in *some* fashion rather than that they be deter-

---

2 Judges make rules of law. On the "will" theory this is an
encroachment on the legislative function. Not so, if the judges
further define conditions of action.

mined by some inherent principle to be just such and such. In other words, within limits it is indifferent what results are fixed by the conditions settled upon; what is important is that the consequences be certain enough to be predictable. The rule of the road is typical of a large number of rules. So is the fixing of sunset or of a specified hour as the exact time when the felonious entering of the premises of another takes on a more serious quality. On the other hand, rules of law are reasonable so that "reason" is appealed to by some as their fount and origin on the ground pointed out by Hume.[3] Men are naturally shortsighted, and the shortsightedness is increased and perverted by the influence of appetite and passion. "The law" formulates remote and long-run consequences. It then operates as a condensed available check on the naturally overweening influence of immediate desire and interest over decision. It is a means of doing for a person what otherwise only his own foresight, if thoroughly reasonable, could do. For a rule of law, although it may be laid down because of a special act as its occasion, is formulated in view of an indefinite variety of other possible acts. It is necessarily a generalization; for it is generic as to the predictable consequences of a *class* of facts. If the incidents of a particular occasion exercise undue influence upon the content of a rule of law, it will soon be

[3] "A Treatise on Human Nature," Part II, sec. vii.

overruled, either explicitly or by neglect. Upon this theory, the law as "embodied reason" means a formulated generalization of means and procedures in behavior which are adapted to secure what is wanted. Reason expresses a function, not a causal origin. Law is reasonable as a man is sensible who selects and arranges conditions adapted to produce the ends he regards as desirable. A recent writer, who regards "reason" as that which generates laws, says, "A debt does not in reason cease to be a debt because time has passed, but the law sets up a limitation. A trespass does not cease in reason to be a trespass because it is indefinitely repeated, yet the law shows a tendency to admit an unresisted trespass in time to the status of right. Time, distance and chance are indifferent to pure reason; but they play their part in the legal order." [4] But if reasonableness is a matter of adaptation of means to consequences, time and distance are things to be given great weight; for they effect both consequences and the ability to foresee them and to act upon them. Indeed, we might select statutes of limitation as excellent examples of the kind of rationality the law contains. Only if reason is looked upon as "pure," that is as a matter of formal logic, do the instances cited manifest limitation of reason.

A third mark of the public organized as a state, a mark which also provides a test of our hypothesis, is

4 Hocking, "Man and the State," p. 51.

that it is concerned with modes of behavior which are old and hence well established, engrained. Invention is a peculiarly personal act, even when a number of persons combine to make something new. A novel idea is the kind of thing that has to occur to somebody in the singular sense. A new project is something to be undertaken and set agoing by private initiative. The newer an idea or plan, the more it deviates from what is already recognized and established in practice. By the nature of the case an innovation is a departure from the customary. Hence the resistance it is likely to encounter. We, to be sure, live in an era of discoveries and inventions. Speaking generically, innovation itself has become a custom. Imagination is wonted to it; it is expected. When novelties take the form of mechanical appliances, we incline to welcome them. But this is far from always having been the case. The rule has been to look with suspicion and greet with hostility the appearance of anything new, even a tool or utensil. For an innovation *is* a departure, and one which brings in its train some incalculable disturbance of the behavior to which we have grown used and which seems "natural." As a recent writer has clearly shown, inventions have made their way insidiously; and because of some immediate convenience. If their effects, their long-run consequences, in altering habits of behavior had been foreseen, it is safe to say that most of them would have been destroyed as wicked, just as many of them were retarded in adoption because they were felt to be sacrilegious.[5] In any case, we cannot think of their invention being the work of the state.[6]

The organized community is still hesitant with reference to new ideas of a non-technical and non-technological nature. They are felt to be disturbing to social behavior; and rightly so, as far as old and established behavior is concerned. Most persons object to having their habits unsettled, their habits of belief no less than habits of overt action. A new idea *is* an unsettling of received beliefs; otherwise, it would not be a new idea. This is only to say that the production of new ideas is peculiarly a private performance. About the most we can ask of the state, judging from states which have so far existed, is that it put up with their production by private individuals without undue meddling. A state which will organize to manufacture and disseminate new ideas and new ways of thinking may come into existence some time, but such a state is a matter of faith, not sight. When it comes it will arrive because the beneficial consequences of new ideas have become an article of common faith and repute. It may, indeed, be said that even now the state provides those condi-

[5] Ayers, "Science: The False Messiah," Chapter IV, The Lure of Machinery.

[6] The one obvious exception concerns the tools of waging war. With respect to them, the state has often shown itself as greedy as it has been reluctant and behindhand with reference to other inventions.

tions of security which are necessary if private persons are to engage effectually in discovery and invention. But this service is a by-product; it is foreign to the grounds on which the conditions in question are maintained by the public. And it must be offset by noting the extent to which the state of affairs upon which the public heart is most set is unfavorable to thinking in other than technical lines. In any case, it is absurd to expect the public, because it is called in no matter how eulogistic a sense the state, to rise above the intellectual level of its average constituents.

When, however, a mode of behavior has become old and familiar, and when an instrumentality has come into use as a matter of course, provided it is a prerequisite of other customary pursuits, it tends to come within the scope of the state. An individual may make his own track in a forest; but highways are usually public concerns. Without roads which one is free to use at will, men might almost as well be castaways on a desert island. Means of transit and communication affect not only those who utilize them but all who are dependent in any way upon what is transported, whether as producers or consumers. The increase of easy and rapid intercommunication means that production takes place more and more for distant markets and it puts a premium upon mass-production. Thus it becomes a disputed question whether railroads as well as highways should not be administered by public officials, and in any case some measure

of official regulation is instituted, as they become
settled bases of social life.

The tendency to put what is old and established in
uniform lines under the regulation of the state has
psychological support. Habits economize intellectual
as well as muscular energy. They relieve the mind
from thought of means, thus freeing thought to deal
with new conditions and purposes. Moreover, interference with a well-established habit is followed by un-
easiness and antipathy. The efficiency of liberation
from attention to whatever is regularly recurrent is re-
enforced by an emotional tendency to get rid of bother.
Hence there is a general disposition to turn over activities which have become highly standardized and uniform to representatives of the public. It is possible
that the time will come when not only railways will have
become routine in their operation and management, but
also existing modes of machine production, so that business men instead of opposing public ownership will
clamor for it in order that they may devote their energies to affairs which involve more novelty, variation and
opportunities for risk and gain. They might conceiv-
ably, even under a régime of continued private property in general, no more wish to be bothered with routin-
ized operations than they would want to take over the
care of public streets. Even now the question of the
public's taking charge of the machinery of the manufacture of goods is less a matter of wholesale "individualism" versus "socialism" than it is of the ratio of the

experimental and novel in their management to the
habitual and matter-of-course; of that which is taken
for granted as a condition of other things to that
which is significant in its own operation.

A fourth mark of the public is indicated by the idea
that children and other dependents (such as the insane,
the permanently helpless) are peculiarly its wards.
When the parties involved in any transaction are un-
equal in status, the relationship is likely to be one-
sided, and the interests of one party to suffer. If the
consequences appear serious, especially if they seem to
be irretrievable, the public brings to bear a weight that
will equalize conditions. Legislatures are more ready to
regulate the hours of labor of children than of adults,
of women than of men. In general, labor legislation is
justified against the charge that it violates liberty of
contract on the ground that the economic resources of
the parties to the arrangement are so disparate that
the conditions of a genuine contract are absent; action by the state is introduced to form a level on which
bargaining takes place. Labor unions often object,
however, to such "paternalistic" legislation on the
ground that voluntary combinations to ensure collective
bargaining is better for those concerned than action
taken without the active participation of laborers. The
general objection that paternalism tends to keep those
affected by it permanently in the status of children,
without an impetus to help themselves, rests on the
same basis. The difference here is nevertheless not as

to the principle that inequality of status may call for public intervention, but as to the best means of securing and maintaining equality.

There has been a steady tendency for the education of children to be regarded as properly a state charge in spite of the fact that children are primarily the care of a family. But the period in which education is possible to an effective degree is that of childhood; if this time is not taken advantage of the consequences are irreparable. The neglect can rarely be made up later. In the degree, then, that a certain measure of instruction and training is deemed to have significant consequences for the social body, rules are laid down affecting the action of parents in relation to their children, and those who are not parents are taxed—Herbert Spencer to the contrary notwithstanding—to maintain schools. Again, the consequences of neglect of safeguards in industries involving machines which are dangerous and those presenting unhygienic conditions, are so serious and irretrievable that the modern public has intervened to maintain conditions conducive to safety and health. Movements which aim at insurance against illness and old-age under governmental auspices illustrate the same principle. While public regulation of a minimum wage is still a disputed matter, the argument in behalf of it appeals to the criterion stated. The argument in effect is that a living wage is a matter of such serious indirect consequences to society that it cannot be safely left to the parties directly concerned, owing to the fact that immediate need may incapacitate one party to the transaction from effective bargaining.

In what has been said there is no attempt to lay down criteria to be applied in a predetermined way to ensure just such and such results. We are not concerned to predict the special forms which state action will take in the future. We have simply been engaged in pointing out the marks by which public action as distinct from private is characterized. Transactions between singular persons and groups bring a public into being when their indirect consequences—their effects beyond those immediately engaged in them—are of importance. Vagueness is not eliminated from the idea of importance. But at least we have pointed out some of the factors which go to make up importance: namely, the far-reaching character of consequences, whether in space or time; their settled, uniform and recurrent nature, and their irreparableness. Each one of these matters involves questions of degree. There is no sharp and clear line which draws itself, pointing out beyond peradventure, like the line left by a receding high tide, just where a public comes into existence which has interests so significant that they must be looked after and administered by special agencies, or governmental officers. Hence there is often room for dispute. The line of demarcation between actions left to private initiative and management and those regulated by the state has to be discovered experimentally.

As we shall see later, there are assignable reasons why it will be drawn very differently at different times and places. The very fact that the public depends upon consequences of acts and the perception of consequences, while its organization into a state depends upon the ability to invent and employ special instrumentalities, shows how and why publics and political institutions differ widely from epoch to epoch and from place to place. To suppose that an *a priori* conception of the intrinsic nature and limits of the individual on one side and the state on the other will yield good results once for all is absurd. If, however, the state has a definite nature, as it should have if it were formed by fixed causal agencies, or if individuals have a nature fixed once for all apart from conditions of association, a final and wholesale partitioning of the realms of personal and state activity is the logical conclusion. The failure of such a theory to reach practical solutions is, therefore, a further confirmation of the theory which emphasizes the consequences of activity as the essential affair.

In conclusion, we shall make explicit what has been implied regarding the relation to one another of public, government and state.[7] There have been two extreme

[7] This is a convenient place for making explicit a qualification which has to be understood throughout but which is slighted in the text. The words "government" and "officers" are taken

views about this point. On one hand, the state has been identified with government. On the other hand, the state, having a necessary existence of its own, *per se*, is said then to proceed to form and employ certain agencies forming government, much as a man hires servants and assigns them duties. The latter view is appropriate when the causal agency theory is relied upon. Some force, whether a general will or the singular wills of assembled individuals, calls the state into being. Then the latter as a secondary operation chooses certain persons through whom to act. Such a theory helps those who entertain it to retain the

functionally, not in terms of some particular structure which is so familiar to us that it leaps to the eyes when these words are used. Both words in their functional meaning are much wider in application than what is meant when we speak, say, of the government and officers of Great Britain or the United States. In households, for example, there have usually been rule and "heads"; the parents, for most purposes the father, have been officers of the family interest. The "patriarchal family" presents an emphatic intensification, on account of comparative isolation of the household from other social forms, of what exists in lesser degree in almost all families. The same sort of remark applies to the use of the term "states," in connection with publics. The text is concerned with modern conditions, but the hypothesis propounded is meant to hold good generally. So to the patent objection that the state is a very modern institution, it is replied that while modernity is a property of those *structures* which go by the name of states, yet all history, or almost all, records the exercise of analogous *functions*. The argument concerns these functions and the mode of their operation, no matter what word be used, though for the sake of brevity the word "state," like the words "government" and "officer," has been freely employed.

idea of the inherent sanctity of the state. Concrete
political evils such as history exhibits in abundance
can be laid at the door of fallible and corrupt governments, while the state keeps its honor unbesmirched.
The identification of the state with government has the
advantage of keeping the mind's eye upon concrete and
observable facts; but it involves an unaccountable separation between rulers and people. If a government
exists by itself and on its own account, why should
there be government? Why should there persist the
habits of loyalty and obedience which permit it to
rule?

The hypothesis which has been advanced frees
us from the perplexities which cluster about both of
these two notions. The lasting, extensive and serious
consequences of associated activity bring into existence
a public. In itself it is unorganized and formless. By
means of officials and their special powers it becomes
a state. A public articulated and operating through
representative officers is the state; there is no state
without a government, but also there is none without
the public. The officers are still singular beings, but
they exercise new and special powers. These may be
turned to their private account. Then government is
corrupt and arbitrary. Quite apart from deliberate
graft, from using unusual powers for private glorification and profit, density of mind and pomposity of behavior, adherence to class-interest and its prejudices,
are strengthened by position. "Power is poison" was

the remark of one of the best, shrewdest and most experienced observers of Washington politicians. On the other hand, occupancy of office may enlarge a man's views and stimulate his social interest so that he exhibits as a statesman traits foreign to his private life.

But since the public forms a state only by and through officials and their acts, and since holding official position does not work a miracle of transubstantiation, there is nothing perplexing nor even discouraging in the spectacle of the stupidities and errors of political behavior. The facts which give rise to the spectacle should, however, protect us from the illusion of expecting extraordinary change to follow from a mere change in political agencies and methods. Such a change sometimes occurs, but when it does, it is because the social conditions, in generating a new public, have prepared the way for it; the state sets a formal seal upon forces already in operation by giving them a defined channel through which to act. Conceptions of "The State" as something *per se*, something intrinsically manifesting a general will and reason, lend themselves to illusions. They make such a sharp distinction between *the* state and *a* government that, from the standpoint of the theories, a government may be corrupt and injurious and yet The State by the same idea retain its inherent dignity and nobility. Officials may be mean, obstinate, proud and stupid and yet the nature of the state which they serve remain essentially unimpaired. Since, however, a public is organized into a state through its government, the state is as its officials are. Only through constant watchfulness and criticism of public officials by citizens can a state be maintained in integrity and usefulness.

The discussion also returns with some added illumination to the problem of the relation of state and society. The problem of the relation of individuals to associations—sometimes posed as the relation of *the* individual to society—is a meaningless one. We might as well make a problem out of the relation of the letters of an alphabet to the alphabet. An alphabet *is* letters, and "society" is individuals in their connections with one another. The mode of combination of letters with one another is obviously a matter of importance; letters form words and sentences when combined, and have no point nor sense except in some combination. I would not say that the latter statement applies literally to individuals, but it cannot be gainsaid that singular human beings exist and behave in constant and varied association with one another. These modes of conjoint action and their consequences profoundly affect not only the outer habits of singular persons, but their dispositions in emotion, desire, planning and valuing.

"Society," however, is either an abstract or a collective noun. In the concrete, there are societies, associations, groups of an immense number of kinds, having different ties and instituting different interests. They may be gangs, criminal bands; clubs for sport, sociabil-

ity and eating; scientific and professional organizations; political parties and unions within them; families; religious denominations, business partnerships and
corporations; and so on in an endless list. The associations may be local, nation-wide and trans-national.
Since there is no one *thing* which may be called society,
except their indefinite overlapping, there is no unqualified eulogistic connotation adhering to the term "society." Some societies are in the main to be approved;
some to be condemned, on account of their consequences
upon the character and conduct of those engaged in
them and because of their remoter consequences upon
others. All of them, like all things human, are mixed
in quality; "society" is something to be approached
and judged critically and discriminatingly. "Sociali-
zation" of some sort—that is, the reflex modification of
wants, beliefs and work because of share in a united
action—is inevitable. But it is as marked in the formation of frivolous, dissipated, fanatical, narrow-
minded and criminal persons as in that of competent
inquirers, learned scholars, creative artists and good
neighbors.

Confining our notice to the results which are desirable, it appears that there is no reason for assigning
all the values which are generated and maintained by
means of human associations to the work of states. Yet
the same unbridled generalizing and fixating tendency
of the mind which leads to a monistic fixation of society
has extended beyond the hypostatizing of "society"

and produced a magnified idealization of The State.
All values which result from any kind of association
are habitually imputed by one school of social philosophers to the state.   Naturally the result is to place
the state beyond criticism.   Revolt against the state
is then thought to be the one unforgivable social sin.
Sometimes the deification proceeds from a special need
of the time, as in the cases of Spinoza and Hegel.
Sometimes it springs from a prior belief in universal
will and reason and a consequent need of finding some
empirical phenomena which may be identified with the
externalization of this absolute spirit.   Then this is
employed, by circular logic, as evidence for the existence of such a spirit.   The net import of our discussion
is that a state is a distinctive and secondary form of
association, having a specifiable work to do and specified organs of operation.

It is quite true that most states, after they have
been brought into being, react upon the primary groupings.   When a state is a good state, when the officers
of the public genuinely serve the public interests, this
reflex effect is of great importance.   It renders the
desirable associations solider and more coherent; indirectly it clarifies their aims and purges their activities.   It places a discount upon injurious groupings
and renders their tenure of life precarious.   In per-
forming these services, it gives the individual members
of valued associations greater liberty and security: it
relieves them of hampering conditions which if they had

to cope with personally would absorb their energies in mere negative struggle against evils. It enables individual members to count with reasonable certainty upon what others will do, and thus facilitates mutually helpful coöperations. It creates respect for others and for one's self. A measure of the goodness of a state is the degree in which it relieves individuals from the waste of negative struggle and needless conflict and confers upon him positive assurance and reënforcement in what he undertakes. This is a great service, and there is no call to be niggardly in acknowledging the transformations of group and personal action which states have historically effected.

But this recognition cannot be legitimately converted into the monopolistic absorption of all associations into The State, nor of all social values into political value. The all-inclusive nature of the state signifies only that officers of the public (including, of course, law-makers) may act so as to fix conditions under which *any* form of association operates; its comprehensive character refers only to the impact of its behavior. A war like an earthquake may "include" in its consequences all elements in a given territory, but the inclusion is by way of effects, not by inherent nature or right. A beneficent law, like a condition of general economic prosperity, may favorably affect all interests in a particular region, but it cannot be called a whole of which the elements influenced are parts. Nor can the liberating and confirming results of public

action be construed to yield a wholesale idealization
of states in contrast with other associations. For
state activity is often injurious to the latter. One of
the chief occupations of states has been the waging of
war and the suppression of dissentient minorities.
Moreover, their action, even when benign, presupposes
values due to non-political forms of living together
which are but extended and reënforced by the public
through its agents.

The hypothesis which we have supported has obvious
points of contact with what is known as the pluralistic
conception of the state. It presents also a marked
point of difference. Our doctrine of plural forms is a
statement of a fact: that there exist a plurality of
social groupings, good, bad and indifferent. It is not
a doctrine which prescribes inherent limits to state
action. It does not intimate that the function of the
state is limited to settling conflicts among other groups,
as if each one of them had a fixed scope of action of
its own. Were that true, the state would be only an
umpire to avert and remedy trespasses of one group
upon another. Our hypothesis is neutral as to any
general, sweeping implications as to how far state activity may extend. It does not indicate any particular
polity of public action. At times, the consequences of
the conjoint behavior of some persons may be such that
a large public interest is generated which can be
fulfilled only by laying down conditions which involve
a large measure of reconstruction within that group.

There is no more an inherent sanctity in a church, trade-union, business corporation, or family institution than there is in the state. Their value is also to be measured by their consequences. The consequences vary with concrete conditions; hence at one time and place a large measure of state activity may be indicated and at another time a policy of quiescence and *laissez-faire*. Just as publics and states vary with conditions of time and place, so do the concrete functions which should be carried on by states. There is no antecedent universal proposition which can be laid down because of which the functions of a state should be limited or should be expanded. Their scope is something to be critically and experimentally determined.

CHAPTER III

THE DEMOCRATIC STATE

Singular persons are the foci of action, mental and moral, as well as overt. They are subject to all kinds of social influences which determine *what* they can think of, plan and choose. The conflicting streams of social influence come to a single and conclusive issue only in personal consciousness and deed. When a public is generated, the same law holds. It arrives at decisions, makes terms and executes resolves only through the medium of individuals. They are officers; they represent a Public, but the Public acts only through them. We say in a country like our own that legislators and executives are elected by the public. The phrase might appear to indicate that the Public acts. But, after all, individual men and women exercise the franchise; the public is here a collective name for a multitude of persons each voting as an anonymous unit. As a citizen-voter each one of these persons is, however, an officer of the public. He expresses his will as a representative of the public interest as much so as does a senator or sheriff. His vote may express his hope to profit in private purse by the election of some man or the ratification of some proposed law. He may fail, in other words, in effort to represent the interest entrusted to him. But in this respect he does not differ from those explicitly designated public officials who have also been known to betray the interest committed to them instead of faithfully representing it.

In other words, every officer of the public, whether he represents it as a voter or as a stated official, has a dual capacity. From this fact the most serious problem of government arises. We commonly speak of some governments as representative in contrast with others which are not. By our hypothesis all governments are representative in that they purport to stand for the interests which a public has in the behavior of individuals and groups. There is, however, no contradiction here. Those concerned in government are still human beings. They retain their share of the ordinary traits of human nature. They still have private interests to serve and interests of special groups, those of the family, clique or class to which they belong. Rarely can a person sink himself in his political function; the best which most men attain to is the domination by the public weal of their other desires. What is meant by "representative" government is that the public is definitely organized with the intent to secure this dominance. The dual capacity of every officer of the public leads to conflict in individuals between their genuinely political aims and acts and those which they possess in their non-political rôles. When the public adopts special measures to see to it that the conflict is minimized and that the representative function overrides the private one, political institutions are termed representative.

It may be said that not until recently have publics been conscious that they were publics, so that it is absurd to speak of their organizing themselves to protect and secure their interests. Hence states are a recent development. The facts are, indeed, fatally against attribution of any long history to states provided we use a hard and fast conceptual definition of states. But our definition is founded on the exercise of a function, not on any inherent essence or structural nature. Hence it is more or less a verbal matter just what countries and peoples are called states. What is of importance is that the facts which significantly differentiate various forms from one another be recognized. The objection just urged points to a fact of great significance, whether the word "state" be used or not. It indicates that for long stretches of time the public rôle of rulers has been incidental to other ends for which they have used their powers. There has been a machinery of government, but it has been employed for purposes which in the strict sense are non-political, the deliberate advancement of dynastic interests. Thus we come upon the primary problem of the public: to achieve such recognition of itself as will give it weight in the selection of official representatives and in the definition of their responsibilities and rights. Consideration of this problem leads us, as we shall see, into the discussion of the democratic state.

Taking history as a whole, the selection of rulers
and equipment of them with powers has been a matter
of political accident.   Persons have been selected as
judges, executives and administrators for reasons independent of capacity to serve public interests.   Some
of the Greek states of antiquity and the examination
system of China stand out for the very reason that
they are exceptions to this statement.   History shows
that, in the main, persons have ruled because of some
prerogative and conspicuous place which was independent of their definitively public rôle.   If we introduce the
idea of the public at all, we are bound to say that it
was assumed without question that certain persons
were fit to be rulers because of traits independent of
political considerations.   Thus in many societies the
male elders exercised such rule as obtained in virtue of
the mere fact that they were old men.   Gerontocracy
is a familiar and widespread fact.   Doubtless there
was a presumption that age was a sign of knowledge
of group traditions and of matured experience, but it
can hardly be said that this presumption was consciously the influential factor in giving old men a
monopoly of rule.   Rather they had it *ipso facto*, because they had it.   A principle of inertia, of least resistance and least action, operated.   Those who were
already conspicuous in some respect, were it only for
long gray beards, had political powers conferred upon
them.

Success in military achievement is an irrelevant fac-

tor which has controlled the selection of men to rule.
Whether or no "camps are the true mothers of cities,"
whether or no Herbert Spencer was right in declaring
that government originated in chieftainship for war
purposes, there is no doubt that, in most communities,
the ability of a man to win battles has seemed to mark
him out as a predestined manager of the civil affairs
of a community. There is no need to argue that the
two positions demand different gifts, and that achievement in one is no proof of fitness for the other. The
fact remains. Nor do we have to look at ancient states
for evidence of its effective operation. States nominally democratic show the same tendency to assume
that a winning general has some quasi-divine appointment to political office. Reason would teach that oftentimes even the politicians who are most successful
in instigating the willingness of the civilian population
to support a war are by that very fact incapacitated
for the offices of making a just and enduring peace.
But the treaty of Versailles is there to show how difficult it is to make a shift of personnel even when conditions radically alter so that there is need for men of a
changed outlook and interests. To those who have, it
shall be given. It is human nature to think along the
easiest lines, and this induces men when they want
conspicuous leaders in the civil function to fasten upon
those who are already conspicuous, no matter what
the reason.

Aside from old men and warriors, medicine men and

priests have had a ready-made, predestined vocation to rule. Where the community welfare is precarious and dependent upon the favor of supernatural beings, those skilled in the arts by which the wrath and jealousy of the gods are averted and their favor procured, have the marks of superior capacity to administer states. Success in living to an old age, in battle and in occult arts, have, however, been most signalized in the *initiation* of political régimes. What has counted most in the long run is the dynastic factor. *Beati possidentes.* The family from which a ruler has been taken occupies in virtue of that fact a conspicuous position and superior power. Preëminence in status is readily taken for excellence. Divine favor *ex officio* attends a family in which rule has been exercised for enough generations so that the memory of original exploits has grown dim or become legendary. The emoluments, pomp and power which go with rule are not thought to need justification. They not only embellish and dignify it, but are regarded as symbols of intrinsic worthiness to possess it. Custom consolidates what accident may have originated; established power has a way of legitimizing itself. Alliances with other potent families within and without the country, possession of large landed estates, a retinue of courtiers and access to revenues of the state, with a multitude of other things irrelevant to the public interest, establish a dynastic position at the same time that they divert the genuine political function to private ends.

An additional complication is introduced because the glory, wealth and power of rulers constitutes in itself an invitation to seize and exploit office. The causes which operate to induce men to strive for any shining object operate with increased appeal in the case of governmental power. The centralization and scope of functions which are needed in order to serve the interests of the public become, in other words, seductions to draw state officials into subserving private ends. All history shows how difficult it is for human beings to bear effectually in mind the objects for the nominal sake of which they are clothed with power and pomp; it shows the ease with which they employ their panoply to advance private and class interests. Were actual dishonesty the only, or even chief, foe, the problem would be much simpler. The ease of routine, the difficulty of ascertaining public needs, the intensity of the glare which attends the seat of the mighty, desire for immediate and visible results, play the larger part. One often hears it said by socialists justly impatient with the present economic régime that "industry should be taken out of private hands." One recognizes what they intend: that it should cease to be regulated by desire for private profit and should function for the benefit of producers and consumers, instead of being sidetracked to the advantage of financiers and stockholders. But one wonders whether those who so readily utter this saying have asked themselves into whose hands industry is to pass? Into those of the public?

But, alas, the public has no hands except those of individual human beings. The essential problem is that of transforming the action of such hands so that it will be animated by regard for social ends. There is no magic by which this result can be accomplished. The same causes which have led men to utilize concentrated political power to serve private purposes will continue to act to induce men to employ concentrated economic power in behalf of non-public aims. This fact does not imply the problem is insoluble. But it indicates where the problem resides, whatever guise it assumes. Since officers of the public have a dual make-up and capacity, what conditions and what technique are necessary in order that insight, loyalty and energy may be enlisted on the side of the public and political rôle?

These commonplace considerations have been adduced as a background for discussion of the problems and prospects of democratic government. Democracy is a word of many meanings. Some of them are of such a broad social and moral import as to be irrelevant to our immediate theme. But one of the meanings is distinctly political, for it denotes a mode of government, a specified practice in selecting officials and regulating their conduct as officials. This is not the most inspiring of the different meanings of democracy; it is comparatively special in character. But it contains about all that is relevant to *political* democracy. Now the theories and practices regarding the selection and behavior of public officials which constitute political democracy have been worked out against the historical background just alluded to. They represent an effort in the first place to counteract the forces that have so largely determined the possession of rule by accidental and irrelevant factors, and in the second place an effort to counteract the tendency to employ political power to serve private instead of public ends. To discuss democratic government at large apart from its historic background is to miss its point and to throw away all means for an intelligent criticism of it. In taking the distinctively historical point of view we do not derogate from the important and even superior claims of democracy as an ethical and social ideal. We limit the topic for discussion in such a way as to avoid "the great bad," the mixing of things which need to be kept distinct.

Viewed as a historical tendency exhibited in a chain of movements which have affected the forms of government over almost the entire globe during the last century and a half, democracy is a complex affair. There is a current legend to the effect that the movement originated in a single clear-cut idea, and has proceeded by a single unbroken impetus to unfold itself to a predestined end, whether triumphantly glorious or fatally catastrophic. The myth is perhaps rarely held in so simple and unmixed a form. But something approaching it is found whenever men either praise or damn democratic government absolutely, that is, with-

out comparing it with alternative polities. Even the
least accidental, the most deliberately planned, political
forms do not embody some absolute and unquestioned
good. They represent a choice, amid a complex of
contending forces, of that particular possibility which
appears to promise the most good with the least attend-
ant evil.

Such a statement, moreover, immensely oversimpli-
fies. Political forms do not originate in a once for all
way. The greatest change, once it is accomplished, is
simply the outcome of a vast series of adaptations and
responsive accommodations, each to its own particular
situation. Looking back, it is possible to make out a
trend of more or less steady change in a single direction. But it is, we repeat, mere mythology to attribute
such unity of result as exists (which is always easy
to exaggerate) to single force or principle. Political
democracy has emerged as a kind of net consequence
of a vast multitude of responsive adjustments to a vast
number of situations, no two of which were alike, but
which tended to converge to a common outcome. The
democratic convergence, moreover, was not the result
of distinctively political forces and agencies. Much
less is democracy the product *of* democracy, of some
inherent nisus, or immanent idea. The temperate generalization to the effect that the unity of the democratic movement is found in effort to remedy evils experienced in consequence of prior political institutions
realizes that it proceeded step by step, and that each

step was taken without foreknowledge of any ultimate
result, and, for the most part, under the immediate influence of a number of differing impulses and slogans.

It is even more important to realize that the conditions out of which the efforts at remedy grew and which
it made possible for them to succeed were primarily
non-political in nature.   For the evils were of long
standing, and any account of the movement must raise
two questions: Why were efforts at improvement not
made earlier, and, when they were made, why did they
take just the form which they did take? The answers
to both questions will be found in distinctive religious,
scientific and economic changes which finally took effect
in the political field, being themselves primarily non-
political and innocent of democratic intent.   Large
questions and far-ranging ideas and ideals arose during
the course of the movement. But theories of the nature
of the individual and his rights, of freedom and authority, progress and order, liberty and law, of the common
good and a general will, of democracy itself, did not
produce the movement. They reflected it in thought;
after they emerged, they entered into subsequent striv-
ings and had practical effect.

We have insisted that the development of political
democracy represents the convergence of a great number of social movements, no one of which owed either
its origin or its impetus to inspiration of democratic
ideals or to planning for the eventual outcome. This
fact makes irrelevant both pæans and condemnations

based upon conceptual interpretations of democracy, which, whether true or false, good or bad, are reflections of facts in thought, not their causal authors. In any case, the complexity of the historic events which have operated is such as to preclude any thought of rehearsing them in these pages, even if I had a knowledge and competency which are lacking. Two general and obvious considerations need, however, to be mentioned. Born in revolt against established forms of government and the state, the events which finally culminated in democratic political forms were deeply tinged by fear of government, and were actuated by a desire to reduce it to a minimum so as to limit the evil it could do.

Since established political forms were tied up with other institutions, especially ecclesiastical, and with a solid body of tradition and inherited belief, the revolt also extended to the latter. Thus it happened that the intellectual terms in which the movement expressed itself had a negative import even when they seemed to be positive. Freedom presented itself as an end in itself, though it signified in fact liberation from oppression and tradition. Since it was necessary, upon the intellectual side, to find justification for the movements of revolt, and since established authority was upon the side of institutional life, the natural recourse was appeal to some inalienable sacred authority resident in the protesting individuals. Thus "individualism" was born, a theory which endowed singular persons in isolation from any associations, except those which they deliberately formed for their own ends, with native or natural rights. The revolt against old and limiting associations was converted, intellectually, into the doctrine of independence of any and all associations.

Thus the practical movement for the limitation of the powers of government became associated, as in the influential philosophy of John Locke, with the doctrine that the ground and justification of the restriction was prior non-political rights inherent in the very structure of the individual. From these tenets, it was a short step to the conclusion that the sole end of government was the protection of individuals in the rights which were theirs by nature. The American revolution was a rebellion against an established government, and it naturally borrowed and expanded these ideas as the ideological interpretation of the effort to obtain independence of the colonies. It is now easy for the imagination to conceive circumstances under which revolts against prior governmental forms would have found its theoretical formulation in an assertion of the rights of groups, of other associations than those of a political nature. There was no logic which rendered necessary the appeal to the individual as an independent and isolated being. In abstract logic, it would have sufficed to assert that some primary groupings had claims which the state could not legitimately encroach upon. In that case, the celebrated modern antithesis of the Individual and Social, and the problem of their reconciliation, would not have arisen. The problem would have taken the form of defining the relationship which non-political groups bear to political union. But, as we have already remarked, the obnoxious state was closely bound up in fact and in tradition with other associations, ecclesiastic (and through its influence with the family), and economic, such as gilds and corporations, and, by means of the church-state, even with unions for scientific inquiry and with educational institutions. The easiest way out was to go back to the naked individual, to sweep away all associations as foreign to his nature and rights save as they proceeded from his own voluntary choice, and guaranteed his own private ends.

Nothing better exhibits the scope of the movement than the fact that philosophic theories of knowledge made the same appeal to the self, or ego, in the form of personal consciousness identified with mind itself, that political theory made to the natural individual, as the court of ultimate resort. The schools of Locke and Descartes, however much they were opposed in other respects, agreed in this, differing only as to whether the sentient or rational nature of the individual was the fundamental thing. From philosophy the idea crept into psychology, which became an introspective and introverted account of isolated and ultimate private consciousness. Henceforth moral and political individualism could appeal to "scientific" warrant for its tenets and employ a vocabulary made current by psy-

chology:—although in fact the psychology appealed
to as its scientific foundation was its own offspring.

The "individualistic" movement finds a classic expression in the great documents of the French Revolution, which at one stroke did away with all forms of
association, leaving, in theory, the bare individual face
to face with the state. It would hardly have reached
this point, however, if it had not been for a second
factor, which must be noted. A new scientific movement had been made possible by the invention and
use of new mechanical appliances—the lens is typical—
which focused attention upon tools like the lever and
pendulum, which, although they had long been in use,
had not formed points of departure for scientific theory.
This new development in inquiry brought, as Bacon
foretold, great economic changes in its wake. It more
than paid its debt to tools by leading to the invention
of machines. The use of machinery in production and
commerce was followed by the creation of new powerful
social conditions, personal opportunities and wants.
Their adequate manifestation was limited by established political and legal practices. The legal regulations so affected every phase of life which was interested
in taking advantage of the new economic agencies as
to hamper and oppress the free play of manufacture
and exchange. The established custom of states, expressed intellectually in the theory of mercantilism
against which Adam Smith wrote his account of "The
(True) Wealth of Nations," prevented the expansion

of trade between nations, a restriction which reacted
to limit domestic industry.   Internally, there was a
network of restrictions inherited from feudalism.   The
prices of labor and staples were not framed in the
market by higgling but were set by justices of the
peace.   The development of industry was hampered
by laws regulating choice of a calling, apprenticeship,
migration of workers from place to place,—and so on.

Thus fear of government and desire to limit its operations, because they were hostile to the development
of the new agencies of production and distribution
of services and commodities, received powerful reënforcement.   The economic movement was perhaps the
more influential because it operated, not in the name
of the individual and his inherent rights, but in the
name of Nature.   Economic "laws," that of labor
springing from natural wants and leading to the creation of wealth, of present abstinence in behalf of future
enjoyment leading to creation of capital effective in
piling up still more wealth, the free play of competitive
exchange, designated the law of supply and demand,
were "natural" laws.   They were set in opposition to
political laws as artificial, man-made affairs.   The inherited tradition which remained least questioned was
a conception of Nature which made Nature something
to conjure with.   The older metaphysical conception
of Natural Law was, however, changed into an economic conception; laws of nature, implanted in human
nature, regulated the production and exchange of goods

and services, and in such a way that when they were
kept free from artificial, that is political, meddling, they
resulted in the maximum possible social prosperity and
progress. Popular opinion is little troubled by questions of logical consistency. The economic theory of
laissez-faire, based upon belief in beneficent natural
laws which brought about harmony of personal profit
and social benefit, was readily fused with the doctrine
of natural rights. They both had the same practical
import, and what is logic between friends? Thus the
protest of the utilitarian school, which sponsored the
economic theory of natural law in economics, against
natural right theories had no effect in preventing the
popular amalgam of the two sides.

The utilitarian economic theory was such an important factor in developing the theory, as distinct from
the practice, of democratic government that it is worth
while to expound it in outline. Each person naturally
seeks the betterment of his own lot. This can be attained only by industry. Each person is naturally the
best judge of his own interests, and, if left free from
the influence of artificially imposed restrictions, will
express his judgment in his choice of work and exchange of services and goods. Thus, barring accident,
he will contribute to his own happiness in the measure
of his energy in work, his shrewdness in exchange and
his self-denying thrift. Wealth and security are the
natural rewards of economic virtues. At the same
time, the industry, commercial zeal, and ability of in-

dividuals contribute to the social good. Under the invisible hand of a beneficent providence which has framed natural laws, work, capital and trade operate harmoniously to the advantage and advance of men collectively and individually. The foe to be dreaded is interference of government. Political regulation is needed only because individuals accidentally and purposely—since the possession of property by the industrious and able is a temptation to the idle and shiftless—encroach upon one another's activities and properties. This encroachment is the essence of injustice, and the function of government is to secure justice—which signifies chiefly the protection of property and of the contracts which attend commercial exchange. Without the existence of the state men might appropriate one another's property. This appropriation is not only unfair to the laborious individual, but by making property insecure discourages the forthputting of energy at all and thus weakens or destroys the spring of social progress. On the other hand, this doctrine of the function of the state operates automatically as a limit imposed to governmental activities. The state is itself just only when it acts to secure justice— in the sense just defined.

The political problem thus conceived is essentially a problem of discovering and instating a technique which will confine the operations of government as far as may be to its legitimate business of protecting economic interests, of which the interest a man has in the in-

tegrity of his own life and body is a part. Rulers
share the ordinary cupidity to possess property with
a minimum of personal effort. Left to themselves they
take advantage of the power with which their official
position endows them to levy arbitrarily on the wealth
of others. If they protect the industry and property
of private citizens against the invasions of other private citizens, it is only that they may have more resources upon which to draw for their own ends. The
essential problem of government thus reduces itself to
this: What arrangements will prevent rulers from ad-
vancing their own interests at the expense of the ruled?
Or, in positive terms, by what political means shall the
interests of the governors be identified with those of
the governed?

The answer was given, notably by James Mill, in a
classic formulation of the nature of political democracy. Its significant features were popular election of
officials, short terms of office and frequent elections.
If public officials were dependent upon citizens for official position and its rewards, their personal interests
would coincide with those of people at large—at least
of industrious and property-owning persons. Officials
chosen by popular vote would find their election to
office dependent upon presenting evidence of their zeal
and skill in protecting the interests of the populace.
Short terms and frequent elections would ensure their
being held to regular account; the polling-booth would

constitute their day of judgment. The fear of it would operate as a constant check.

Of course in this account I have oversimplified what was already an oversimplification. The dissertation of James Mill was written before the passage of the Reform Bill of 1832. Taken pragmatically, it was an argument for the extension of the suffrage, then largely in the hands of hereditary landowners, to manufacturers and merchants. James Mill had nothing but dread of pure democracies. He opposed the extension of the franchise to women.[1] He was interested in the new "middle-class" forming under the influence of the application of steam to manufacture and trade. His attitude is well expressed in his conviction that even if the suffrage were extended downwards, the middle-class "which gives to science, art and legislation itself its most distinguished ornaments, and which is the chief source of all that is refined and exalted in human nature, is that portion of the community of which the influence would ultimately decide." In spite, however, of oversimplification, and of its special historic motivation, the doctrine claimed to rest upon universal psychological truth; it affords a fair picture of the principles which were supposed to justify the movement toward democratic government. It is unnecessary to indulge in extensive criticism. The differences between the conditions postulated by the theory and those

[1] This last position promptly called forth a protest from the head of the utilitarian school, Jeremy Bentham.

which have actually obtained with the development of
democratic governments speak for themselves.   The
discrepancy is a sufficient criticism.   This disparity
itself shows, however, that what has happened sprang
from no theory but was inherent in what was going on
not only without respect to theories but without regard
to politics: because, generally speaking, of the use of
steam applied to mechanical inventions.

It would be a great mistake, however, to regard the
idea of the isolated individual possessed of inherent
rights "by nature" apart from association, and the idea
of economic laws as natural, in comparison with which
political laws being artificial are injurious (save when
carefully subordinated), as idle and impotent.   The
ideas were something more than flies on the turning
wheels.   They did not originate the movement toward
popular government, but they did profoundly influence
the forms which it assumed.   Or perhaps it would be
truer to say that persistent older conditions, to which
the theories were more faithful than to the state of
affairs they professed to report, were so reënforced by
the professed philosophy of the democratic state, as to
exercise a great influence.   The result was a skew, a
deflection and distortion, in democratic forms.   Put-
ting the "individualistic" matter in a gross statement,
which has to be corrected by later qualifications, we
may say that "the individual," about which the new
philosophy centered itself, was in process of complete
submergence in fact at the very time in which he was

being elevated on high in theory. As to the alleged subordination of political affairs to natural forces and laws, we may say that actual economic conditions were thoroughly artificial, in the sense in which the theory condemned the artificial. They supplied the man-made instrumentalities by which the new governmental agencies were grasped and used to suit the desires of the new class of business men.

Both of these statements are formal as well as sweeping. To acquire intelligible meaning they must be developed in some detail. Graham Wallas prefixed to the first chapter of his book entitled "The Great Society" the following words of Woodrow Wilson, taken from *The New Freedom:* "Yesterday and ever since history began, men were related to one another as individuals. . . . To-day, the everyday relationships of men are largely with great impersonal concerns, with organizations, not with other individuals. Now this is nothing short of a new social age, a new age of human relationships, a new stage-setting for the drama of life." If we accept these words as containing even a moderate degree of truth, they indicate the enormous ineptitude of the individualistic philosophy to meet the needs and direct the factors of the new age. They suggest what is meant by saying the theory of an individual possessed of desires and claims and endued with foresight and prudence and love of bettering himself was framed at just the time when the individual was counting for less in the direction of social affairs, at a time when mechanical forces and vast impersonal organizations were determining the frame of things.

The statement that "yesterday and even since history began, men were related to one another as individuals" is not true. Men have always been associated together in living, and association in conjoint behavior has affected their relations to one another as individuals. It is enough to recall how largely human relations have been permeated by patterns derived directly and indirectly from the family; even the state was a dynastic affair. But none the less the contrast which Mr. Wilson had in mind is a fact. The earlier associations were mostly of the type well termed by Cooley [2] "face-to-face." Those which were important, which really counted in forming emotional and intellectual dispositions, were local and contiguous and consequently visible. Human beings, if they shared in them at all, shared directly and in a way of which they were aware in both their affections and their beliefs. The state, even when it despotically interfered, was remote, an agency alien to daily life. Otherwise it entered men's lives through custom and common law. No matter how widespread their operation might be, it was not their breadth and inclusiveness which counted but their immediate local presence. The church was indeed both a universal and an intimate affair. But it entered into the life of most human beings not through its uni-

[2] C. H. Cooley, "Social Organization," Ch. iii, on "Primary Groups."

versality, as far as their thoughts and habits were concerned, but through an immediate ministration of rites
and sacraments. The new technology applied in production and commerce resulted in a social revolution.
The local communities without intent or forecast found
their affairs conditioned by remote and invisible organizations. The scope of the latter's activities was so
vast and their impact upon face-to-face associations
so pervasive and unremitting that it is no exaggeration to speak of "a new age of human relations." The
Great Society created by steam and electricity may be
a society, but it is no community. The invasion of the
community by the new and relatively impersonal and
mechanical modes of combined human behavior is the
outstanding fact of modern life. In these ways of
aggregate activity the community, in its strict sense,
is not a conscious partner, and over them it has no
direct control. They were, however, the chief factors
in bringing into being national and territorial states.
The need of some control over them was the chief
agency in making the government of these states democratic or popular in the current sense of these words.

Why, then, was a movement, which involved so much
submerging of personal action in the overflowing consequences of remote and inaccessible collective actions,
reflected in a philosophy of individualism? A complete
answer is out of the question. Two considerations are,
however, obvious and significant. The new conditions
involved a release of human potentialities previously

dormant. While their impact was unsettling to the
community, it was liberating with respect to single
persons, while its oppressive phase was hidden in the
impenetrable mists of the future. Speaking with
greater correctness, the oppressive phase affected primarily the elements of the community which were also
depressed in the older and semi-feudal conditions. Since
they did not count for much anyway, being traditionally the drawers of water and hewers of wood, having
emerged only in a legal sense from serfdom, the effect
of new economic conditions upon the laboring masses
went largely unnoted. Day laborers were still in effect,
as openly in the classic philosophy, underlying conditions of community life rather than members of it.
Only gradually did the effect upon them become apparent; by that time they had attained enough power—
were sufficiently important factors in the new economic
régime—to obtain political emancipation, and thus
figure in the forms of the democratic state. Meanwhile
the liberating effect was markedly conspicuous with respect to the members of the "middle-class," the manu-
facturing and mercantile class. It would be short-
sighted to limit the release of powers to opportunities
to procure wealth and enjoy its fruits, although the
creation of material wants and ability to satisfy them
are not to be lightly passed over. Initiative, inventive-
ness, foresight and planning were also stimulated and
confirmed. This manifestation of new powers was on a
sufficiently large scale to strike and absorb attention.

The result was formulated as the discovery of the individual. The customary is taken for granted; it operates subconsciously. Breach of wont and use is focal; it forms "consciousness." The necessary and persistent modes of association went unnoticed. The new ones, which were voluntarily undertaken, occupied thought exclusively. They monopolized the observed horizon. "Individualism" was a doctrine which stated what was focal in thought and purpose.

The other consideration is akin. In the release of new powers singular persons were emancipated from a mass of old habits, regulations and institutions. We have already noted how the methods of production and exchange made possible by the new technology were hampered by the rules and customs of the prior régime. The latter were then felt to be intolerably restrictive and oppressive. Since they hampered the free play of initiative and commercial activity, they were artificial and enslaving. The struggle for emancipation from their influence was identified with the liberty of the individual as such; in the intensity of the struggle, associations and institutions were condemned wholesale as foes of freedom save as they were products of personal agreement and voluntary choice. That many forms of association remained practically untouched was easily overlooked, just because they were matters of course. Indeed, any attempt to touch them, notably the established form of family association and the legal institution of property, were looked upon as subversive, as

license, not liberty, in the sanctified phrase. The identification of democratic forms of government with this
individualism was easy. The right of suffrage represented for the mass a release of hitherto dormant capacity and also, in appearance at least, a power to
shape social relations on the basis of individual volition.

Popular franchise and majority rule afforded the
imagination a picture of individuals in their un-
trammeled individual sovereignty making the state.
To adherents and opponents alike it presented the
spectacle of a pulverizing of established associations
into the desires and intentions of atomic individuals.
The forces, springing from combination and institutional organization which controlled below the surface
the acts which formally issued from individuals, went
unnoted.   It is the essence of ordinary thought to
grasp the external scene and hold it as reality. The
familiar eulogies of the spectacle of "free men" going
to the polls to determine by their personal volitions the
political forms under which they should live is a speci-
men of this tendency to take whatever is readily seen as
the full reality of a situation. In physical matters
natural science has successfully challenged this attitude.   In human matters it remains in almost full
force.

The opponents of popular government were no more
prescient than its supporters, although they showed
more logical sense in following the assumed individualistic premise to its conclusion: the disintegration of

society. Carlyle's savage attacks upon the notion of a society held together only by a "cash-nexus" are well known. Its inevitable terminus to him was "anarchy plus a constable." He did not see that the new industrial régime was forging social bonds as rigid as those which were disappearing and much more extensive—whether desirable ties or not is another matter. Macaulay, the intellectualist of the Whigs, asserted that the extension of suffrage to the masses would surely result in arousing the predatory impulses of the propertyless masses who would use their new political power to despoil the middle as well as upper class. He added that while there was no longer danger that the civilized portions of humanity would be overthrown by the savage and barbarous portions, it was possible that in the bosom of civilization would be engendered the malady which would destroy it.

Incidentally we have trenched upon the other doctrine, the idea that there is something inherently "natural" and amenable to "natural law" in the working of economic forces, in contrast with the man-made artificiality of political institutions. The idea of a natural individual in his isolation possessed of full-fledged wants, of energies to be expended according to his own volition, and of a ready-made faculty of foresight and prudent calculation is as much a fiction in psychology as the doctrine of the individual in possession of antecedent political rights is one in politics. The liberalist school made much of desires, but to them desire was a conscious matter deliberately directed upon a known goal of pleasures. Desire and pleasure were both open and above-board affairs. The mind was seen as if always in the bright sunlight, having no hidden recesses, no unexplorable nooks, nothing underground. Its operations were like the moves in a fair game of chess. They are in the open; the players have nothing up their sleeves; the changes of position take place by express intent and in plain sight; they take place according to rules all of which are known in advance. Calculation and skill, or dullness and inaptitude, determine the result. Mind was "consciousness," and the latter was a clear, transparent, self-revealing medium in which wants, efforts and purposes were exposed without distortion.

To-day it is generally admitted that conduct proceeds from conditions which are largely out of focal attention, and which can be discovered and brought to light only by inquiries more exacting than those which teach us the concealed relationships involved in gross physical phenomena. What is not so generally acknowledged is that the underlying and generative conditions of concrete behavior are social as well as organic: much more social than organic as far as the manifestation of *differential* wants, purposes and methods of operation is concerned. To those who appreciate this fact, it is evident that the desires, aims and standards of satisfaction which the dogma of "natural" economic processes and laws assumes are themselves socially conditioned phenomena. They are reflections into the singular human being of customs and institutions; they are not natural, that is, "native," organic propensities. They mirror a state of civilization. Even more true, if possible, is it that the form in which work is done, industry carried on, is the outcome of accumulated culture, not an original possession of persons in their own structure. There is little that can be called industry and still less that constitutes a store of wealth until tools exist, and tools are the results of slow processes of transmission. The development of tools into machines, the characteristic of the industrial age, was made possible only by taking advantage of science socially accumulated and transmitted. The technique of employing tools and machines was equally something which had to be learned; it was no natural endowment but something acquired by observing others, by instruction and communication.

These sentences are a poor and pallid way of conveying the outstanding fact. There are organic or native needs, of course, as for food, protection and mates. There are innate structures which facilitate them in securing the external objects through which they are met. But the only kind of industry they are capable of giving rise to is a precarious livelihood obtained by gathering such edible plants and animals as chance might throw in the way: the lowest type of savagery just emerging from a brute condition. Nor, strictly speaking, could they effect even this meager result. For because of the phenomenon of helpless infancy even such a primitive régime depends upon the assistance of associated action, including that most valuable form of assistance: learning from others. What would even savage industry be without the use of fire, of weapons, of woven articles, all of which involve communication and tradition? The industrial régime which the authors of "natural" economy contemplated presupposed wants, tools, materials, purposes, techniques and abilities in a thousand ways do pendent upon associated behavior. Thus in the sense in which the authors of the doctrine employed the word "artificial," these things were intensely and cumulatively artificial. What they were really after was a changed direction of custom and institutions. The outcome of the acts of those who were engaged in forwarding the new industry and commerce was a new set of customs and institutions. The latter were as much extensive and enduring conjoint modes of life as were those which they displaced; more so in their sweep and force.

The bearing of this fact upon political theory and practice is evident. Not only were the wants and intentions which actually operated functions of associated life, but they re-determined the forms and temper of this life. Athenians did not buy Sunday newspapers, make investments in stocks and bonds, nor want motor cars. Nor do we to-day want for the most part beautiful bodies and beauty of architectural surroundings. We are mostly satisfied with the result of cosmetics and with ugly slums, and oftentimes with equally ugly palaces. We do not "naturally" or organically need them, but we *want* them. If we do not demand them directly we demand them none the less effectively. For they are necessary consequences of the things upon which we have set our hearts. In other words, a community wants (in the only intelligible sense of wanting, effective demand) either education or ignorance, lovely or squalid surroundings, railway trains or ox-carts, stocks and bonds, pecuniary profit or constructive arts, according as associated activity presents these things to them habitually, esteems them, and supplies the means of attaining them. But that is only half the tale.

Associated behavior directed toward objects which fufill wants not only produces those objects, but brings customs and institutions into being. The indirect and unthought-of consequences are usually more important than the direct. The fallacy of supposing that the new industrial régime would produce just and for the most part only the consequences consciously forecast and aimed at was the counterpart of the fallacy that the wants and efforts characteristic of it were functions of "natural" human beings. They arose out of institutionalized action and they resulted in institutionalized action. The disparity between the results of the industrial revolution and the conscious intentions of those engaged in it is a remarkable case

of the extent to which indirect consequences of conjoint activity outweigh, beyond the possibility of
reckoning, the results directly contemplated. Its outcome was the development of those extensive and invisible bonds, those "great impersonal concerns, organizations," which now pervasively affect the thinking,
willing and doing of everybody, and which have ushered
in the "new era of human relationships."

Equally undreamed of was the effect of the massive
organizations and complicated interactions upon the
state. Instead of the independent, self-moved individuals contemplated by the theory, we have standardized
interchangeable units. Persons are joined together,
not because they have voluntarily chosen to be united
in these forms, but because vast currents are running
which bring men together. Green and red lines, mark-
ing out political boundaries, are on the maps and affect
legislation and jurisdiction of courts, but railways, mails
and telegraph-wires disregard them. The consequences
of the latter influence more profoundly those living
within the legal local units than do boundary lines.
The forms of associated action characteristic of the
present economic order are so massive and extensive
that they determine the most significant constituents
of the public and the residence of power. Inevitably
they reach out to grasp the agencies of government;
they are controlling factors in legislation and administration. Not chiefly because of deliberate and planned
self-interest, large as may be its rôle, but because they

are the most potent and best organized of social forces. In a word, the new forms of combined action due to the modern economic régime control present politics, much as dynastic interests controlled those of two centuries ago. They affect thinking and desire more than did the interests which formerly moved the state.

We have spoken as if the displacement of old legal and political institutions was all but complete. That is a gross exaggeration. Some of the most fundamental of traditions and habits have hardly been affected at all. It is enough to mention the institution of property. The naïveté with which the philosophy of "natural" economics ignored the effect upon industry and commerce of the legal status of property, the way in which it identified wealth and property in the legal form in which the latter had existed, is almost incredible to-day. But the simple fact is that technological industry has not operated with any great degree of freedom. It has been confined and deflected at every point; it has never taken its own course. The engineer has worked in subordination to the business manager whose primary concern is not with wealth but with the interests of property as worked out in the feudal and semi-feudal period. Thus the one point in which the philosophers of "Individualism" predicted truly was that in which they did not predict at all, but in which they merely clarified and simplified established wont and use: when, that is, they asserted that the main business of government is to make property interests secure.

A large part of the indictments which are now drawn against technological industry are chargeable to the unchanged persistence of a legal institution inherited from the pre-industrial age. It is confusing, however, to identify in a wholesale way this issue with the question of private property. It is conceivable that private property may function socially. It does so even now to a considerable degree. Otherwise it could not be supported for a day. The extent of its social utility is what blinds us to the numerous and great social disutilities that attend its present working, or at least reconcile us to its continuation. The real issue or at least the issue to be first settled concerns the conditions under which the institution of private property legally and politically functions.

We thus reach our conclusion. The same forces which have brought about the forms of democratic government, general suffrage, executives and legislators chosen by majority vote, have also brought about conditions which halt the social and humane ideals that demand the utilization of government as the genuine instrumentality of an inclusive and fraternally associated public. "The new age of human relationships" has no political agencies worthy of it. The democratic public is still largely inchoate and unorganized.

CHAPTER IV

THE ECLIPSE OF THE PUBLIC

Optimism about democracy is to-day under a cloud. We are familiar with denunciation and criticism which, however, often reveal their emotional source in their peevish and undiscriminating tone. Many of them suffer from the same error into which earlier laudations fell. They assume that democracy is the product of an idea, of a single and consistent intent. Carlyle was no admirer of democracy, but in a lucid moment he said: "Invent the printing press and democracy is inevitable." Add to this: Invent the railway, the telegraph, mass manufacture and concentration of population in urban centers, and some form of democratic government is, humanly speaking, inevitable. Political democracy as it exists to-day calls for adverse criticism in abundance. But the criticism is only an exhibition of querulousness and spleen or of a superiority complex, unless it takes cognizance of the conditions out of which popular government has issued. All intelligent political criticism is comparative. It deals not with all-or-none situations, but with practical alternatives; an absolutistic indiscriminate attitude, whether in praise or blame, testifies to the heat of feeling rather than the light of thought.

American democratic polity was developed out of genuine community life, that is, association in local and small centers where industry was mainly agricultural and where production was carried on mainly with hand tools. It took form when English political habits and legal institutions worked under pioneer conditions. The forms of association were stable, even though their units were mobile and migratory. Pioneer conditions put a high premium upon personal work, skill, ingenuity, initiative and adaptability, and upon neighborly sociability. The township or some not much larger area was the political unit, the town meeting the political medium, and roads, schools, the peace of the community, were the political objectives. The state was a sum of such units, and the national state a federation—unless perchance a confederation—of states. The imagination of the founders did not travel far beyond what could be accomplished and understood in a congeries of self-governing communities. The machinery provided for the selection of the chief executive of the federal union is illustrative evidence. The electoral college assumed that citizens would choose men locally known for their high standing; and that these men when chosen would gather together for consultation to name some one known to them for his probity and public spirit and knowledge. The rapidity with which the scheme fell into disuse is evidence of the transitoriness of the state of affairs that was predicated. But at the outset there was no dream of the

time when the very names of the presidential electors
would be unknown to the mass of the voters, when they
would plump for a "ticket" arranged in a more or less
private caucus, and when the electoral college would
be an impersonal registering machine, such that it
would be treachery to employ the personal judgment
which was originally contemplated as the essence of the
affair.

The local conditions under which our institutions
took shape is well indicated by our system, apparently
so systemless, of public education. Any one who has
tried to explain it to a European will understand what
is meant. One is asked, say, what method of administration is followed, what is the course of study and
what the authorized methods of teaching. The American member to the dialogue replies that in this state,
or more likely county, or town, or even some section
of a town called a district, matters stand thus and
thus; somewhere else, so and so. The participant from
this side is perhaps thought by the foreigner to be
engaged in concealing his ignorance; and it would certainly take a veritable cyclopedic knowledge to state
the matter in its entirety. The impossibility of making
any moderately generalized reply renders it almost indispensable to resort to a historical account in order
to be intelligible. A little colony, the members of
which are probably mostly known to one another in
advance, settle in what is almost, or quite, a wilderness.
From belief in its benefits and by tradition, chiefly reli-

gious, they wish their children to know at least how to read, write and figure. Families can only rarely provide a tutor; the neighbors over a certain area, in New England an area smaller even than the township, combine in a "school district." They get a school-house built, perhaps by their own labor, and hire a teacher by means of a committee, and the teacher is paid from the taxes. Custom determines the limited course of study, and tradition the methods of the teacher, modified by whatever personal insight and skill he may bring to bear. The wilderness is gradually subdued; a network of highways, then of railways, unite the previously scattered communities. Large cities grow up; studies grow more numerous and methods more carefully scrutinized. The larger unit, the state, but not the federal state, provides schools for training teachers and their qualifications are more carefully looked into and tested. But subject to certain quite general conditions imposed by the state-legis-lature, but not the national state, local maintenance and control remain the rule. The community pattern is more complicated, but is not destroyed. The in-stance seems richly instructive as to the state of affairs under which our borrowed, English, political institu-tions were reshaped and forwarded.

We have inherited, in short, local town-meeting prac-tices and ideas. But we live and act and have our being in a continental national state. We are held together by non-political bonds, and the political forms are

stretched and legal institutions patched in an *ad hoc*
and improvised manner to do the work they have to
do. Political structures fix the channels in which non-
political, industrialized currents flow. Railways, travel
and transportation, commerce, the mails, telegraph and
telephone, newspapers, create enough similarity of ideas
and sentiments to keep the thing going as a whole, for
they create interaction and interdependence. The unprecedented thing is that states, as distinguished from
military empires, can exist over such a wide area. The
notion of maintaining a unified state, even nominally
self-governing, over a country as extended as the
United States and consisting of a large and racially
diversified population would once have seemed the wild-
est of fancies. It was assumed that such a state could
be found only in territories hardly larger than a city-
state and with a homogeneous population. It seemed
almost self-evident to Plato—as to Rousseau later—
that a genuine state could hardly be larger than the
number of persons capable of personal acquaintance
with one another. Our modern state-unity is due to
the consequences of technology employed so as to facilitate the rapid and easy circulation of opinions and
information, and so as to generate constant and intricate interaction far beyond the limits of face-to-face
communities. Political and legal forms have only piece-
meal and haltingly, with great lag, accommodated themselves to the industrial transformation. The elimination of distance, at the base of which are physical

agencies, has called into being the new form of political association.

The wonder of the performance is the greater because of the odds against which it has been achieved. The stream of immigrants which has poured in is so large and heterogeneous that under conditions which formerly obtained it would have disrupted any semblance of unity as surely as the migratory invasion of alien hordes once upset the social equilibrium of the European continent. No deliberately adopted measures could have accomplished what has actually happened. Mechanical forces have operated, and it is no cause for surprise if the effect is more mechanical than vital. The reception of new elements of population in large number from heterogeneous peoples, often hostile to one another at home, and the welding them into even an outward show of unity is an extraordinary feat. In many respects, the consolidation has occurred so rapidly and ruthlessly that much of value has been lost which different peoples might have contributed. The creation of political unity has also promoted social and intellectual uniformity, a standardization favorable to mediocrity. Opinion has been regimented as well as outward behavior. The temper and flavor of the pioneer have evaporated with extraordinary rapidity; their precipitate, as is often noted, is apparent only in the wild-west romance and the movie. What Bagehot called the cake of custom formed with increasing acceleration, and the cake is

too often flat and soggy.   Mass production is not
confined to the factory.

The resulting political integration has confounded
the expectations of earlier critics of popular government as much as it must surprise its early backers if
they are gazing from on high upon the present scene.
The critics predicted disintegration, instability. They
foresaw the new society falling apart, dissolving into
mutually repellent animated grains of sand.   They,
too, took seriously the theory of "Individualism" as the
basis of democratic government.   A stratification of
society into immemorial classes within which each person performed his stated duties according to his fixed
position seemed to them the only warrant of stability.
They had no faith that human beings released from the
pressure of this system could hold together in any
unity.   Hence they prophesied a flux of governmental
régimes, as individuals formed factions, seized power,
and then lost it as some newly improvised faction
proved stronger.   Had the facts conformed to the
theory of Individualism, they would doubtless have been
right.   But, like the authors of the theory, they ignored
the technological forces making for consolidation.

In spite of attained integration, or rather perhaps because of its nature, the Public seems to be lost; it is certainly bewildered.[1]   The government, officials and their

---

[1] See Walter Lippmann's "The Phantom Public." To this as
well as to his "Public Opinion," I wish to acknowledge my in-
debtedness, not only as to this particular point, but for ideas

activities, are plainly with us. Legislatures make laws
with luxurious abandon; subordinate officials engage in
a losing struggle to enforce some of them; judges on the
bench deal as best they can with the steadily mounting
pile of disputes that come before them. But where is
the public which these officials are supposed to represent? How much more is it than geographical names and
official titles? The United States, the state of Ohio
or New York, the county of this and the city of that?
Is the public much more than what a cynical diplomat
once called Italy: a geographical expression? Just as
philosophers once imputed a substance to qualities and
traits in order that the latter might have something in
which to inhere and thereby gain a conceptual solidity
and consistency which they lacked on their face, so perhaps our political "common-sense" philosophy imputes
a public only to support and substantiate the behavior
of officials. How can the latter be public officers, we
despairingly ask, unless there is a public? If a public
exists, it is surely as uncertain about its own
whereabouts as philosophers since Hume have been
about the residence and make-up of the self. The
number of voters who take advantage of their majestic
right is steadily decreasing in proportion to those who
might use it. The ratio of actual to eligible voters is
now about one-half. In spite of somewhat frantic appeal and organized effort, the endeavor to bring voters

involved in my entire discussion even when it reaches conclusions
diverging from his.

to a sense of their privileges and duties has so far been noted for failure. A few preach the impotence of all politics; the many nonchalantly practice abstinence and indulge in indirect action. Skepticism regarding the efficacy of voting is openly expressed, not only in the theories of intellectuals, but in the words of lowbrow masses: "What difference does it make whether I vote or not? Things go on just the same anyway. My vote never changed anything." Those somewhat more reflective add: "It is nothing but a fight between the ins and the outs. The only difference made by an election is as to who get the jobs, draw the salaries and shake down the plum tree."

Those still more inclined to generalization assert that the whole apparatus of political activities is a kind of protective coloration to conceal the fact that big business rules the governmental roost in any case. Business is the order of the day, and the attempt to stop or deflect its course is as futile as Mrs. Partington essaying to sweep back the tides with a broom. Most of those who hold these opinions would profess to be shocked if the doctrine of economic determinism were argumentatively expounded to them, but they act upon a virtual belief in it. Nor is acceptance of the doctrine limited to radical socialists. It is implicit in the attitude of men of big business and financial interests, who revile the former as destructive "Bolshevists." For it is their firm belief that "prosperity"—a word which has taken on religious color—is the great need of the country, that they are its authors and guardians, and hence by right the determiners of polity. Their denunciations of the "materialism" of socialists is based simply upon the fact that the latter want a different distribution of material force and well-being than that which satisfies those now in control.

The unfitness of whatever public exists, with respect to the government which is nominally its organ, is made manifest in the extra-legal agencies which have grown up. Intermediary groups are closest to the political conduct of affairs. It is interesting to compare the English literature of the eighteenth century regarding factions with the status actually occupied by parties. Factionalism was decried by all thinkers as the chief enemy to political stability. Their voice of condemnation is reëchoed in the writing of early nineteenth-century American writers on politics. Extensive and consolidated factions under the name of parties are now not only a matter of course, but popular imagination can conceive of no other way by which officials may be selected and governmental affairs carried on. The centralizing movement has reached a point where even a third party can lead only a spasmodic and precarious existence. Instead of individuals who in the privacy of their consciousness make choices which are carried into effect by personal volition, there are citizens who have the blessed opportunity to vote for a ticket of men mostly unknown to them, and which is made up for them by an under-cover machine in a caucus whose operations constitute a kind of political predestination. There are those who speak as if ability to choose between two tickets were a high exercise of individual freedom. But it is hardly the kind of liberty contemplated by the authors of the individualistic doctrine. "Nature abhors a vacuum." When the public is as uncertain and obscure as it is to-day, and hence as remote from government, bosses with their political machines fill the void between government and the public. Who pulls the strings which move the bosses and generates power to run the machines is a matter of surmise rather than of record, save for an occasional overt scandal.

Quite aside, however, from the allegation that "Big Business" plays the tune and pulls the strings to which bosses dance, it is true that parties are not creators of policies to any large extent at the present time. For parties yield in piece-meal accommodation to social currents, irrespective of professed principles. As these lines are written a weekly periodical remarks: "Since the end of the Civil War practically all the more important measures which have been embodied in federal legislation have been reached without a national election which turned upon the issue and which divided the two major parties." Reform of civil service, regulation of railways, popular election of senators, national income tax, suffrage for women, and prohibition are supported to substantiate the statement. Hence its other remark appears justified: "American party politics seem at times to be a device for preventing issues which may excite popular feeling and involve bitter controversies from being put up to the American people."

A negatively corroborating fact is seen in the fate of the Child Labor amendment. The need of giving to Congress power to regulate child labor, denied it by decisions of the Supreme Court, had been asserted in the platforms of all political parties; the idea was endorsed by the last three of the presidents belonging to the party in power. Yet so far, the proposed amendment to the constitution has not begun to secure the needed support. Political parties may rule, but they do not govern. The public is so confused and eclipsed that it cannot even use the organs through which it is supposed to mediate political action and polity.

The same lesson is taught by the breakdown of the theory of the responsibility of elected representatives to the electorate, to say nothing of their alleged liability to be called before the bar of the private judgment of individuals. It is at least suggestive that the terms of the theory are best met in legislation of the "pork-barrel" type. There a representative may be called to account for failure to meet local desire, or be rewarded for pertinacity and success in fulfilling its wishes. But only rarely is the theory borne out in important matters, although occasionally it works. But the instances are so infrequent that any skilled political observer could enumerate them by name. The reason for the lack of personal liability to the electorate is evident. The latter is composed of rather amorphous groups. Their political ideas and beliefs are mostly in abeyance between elections. Even in times of political excitement, artificially accelerated, their opinions are moved collectively by the current of the group rather than by independent personal judgment. As a rule, what decides the fate of a person who comes up for election is neither his political excellence nor his political defects. The current runs for or against the party in power and the individual candidate sinks or swims as runs the current. At times there is a general consensus of sentiment, a definite trend in favor of "progressive legislation" or a desire for a "return to normalcy." But even then only exceptional candidates get by on any basis of personal responsibility to the electorate. The "tidal wave" swamps some; the "landslide" carries others into office. At other times, habit, party funds, the skill of managers of the machine, the portrait of a candidate with his firm jaw, his lovely wife and children, and a multitude of other irrelevancies, determine the issue.

These scattered comments are not made in the belief that they convey any novel truth. Such things are familiar; they are the common-places of the political scene. They could be extended indefinitely by any careful observer of the scene. The significant thing is that familiarity has bred indifference if not contempt. Indifference is the evidence of current apathy, and apathy is testimony to the fact that the public is

so bewildered that it cannot find itself. The remarks
are not made with a view to drawing a conclusion.
They are offered with a view to outlining a problem:
What is the public? If there is a public, what are the
obstacles in the way of its recognizing and articulating
itself? Is the public a myth? Or does it come into
being only in periods of marked social transition when
crucial alternative issues stand out, such as that between throwing one's lot in with the conservation of
established institutions or with forwarding new tendencies? In a reaction against dynastic rule which has
come to be felt as despotically oppressive? In a transfer of social power from agrarian classes to industrial?

Is not the problem at the present time that of securing experts to manage administrative matters, other
than the framing of policies? It may be urged that the
present confusion and apathy are due to the fact that
the real energy of society is now directed in all non-
political matters by trained specialists who manage
things, while politics are carried on with a machinery
and ideas formed in the past to deal with quite another
sort of situation. There is no particular public concerned in finding expert school instructors, competent
doctors, or business managers. Nothing called a public
intervenes to instruct physicians in the practice of the
healing art or merchants in the art of salesmanship.
The conduct of these callings and others characteristic
of our time are decided by science and pseudo-science.
The important governmental affairs at present, it may

be argued, are also technically complicated matters to
be conducted properly by experts. And if at present
people are not educated to the recognition of the importance of finding experts and of entrusting administration to them, it may plausibly be asserted that the
prime obstruction lies in the superstitious belief that
there is a public concerned to determine the formation
and execution of general social policies. Perhaps the
apathy of the electorate is due to the irrelevant artificiality of the issues with which it is attempted to work
up factitious excitement. Perhaps this artificiality is
in turn mainly due to the survival of political beliefs
and machinery from a period when science and technology were so immature as not to permit of a definite
technique for handling definite social situations and
meeting specific social needs. The attempt to decide by
law that the legends of a primitive Hebrew people regarding the genesis of man are more authoritative than
the results of scientific inquiry might be cited as a
typical example of the sort of thing which is bound to
happen when the accepted doctrine is that a public
organized for political purposes, rather than experts
guided by specialized inquiry, is the final umpire and
arbiter of issues.

The questions of most concern at present may be
said to be matters like sanitation, public health, health-
ful and adequate housing, transportation, planning of
cities, regulation and distribution of immigrants, selection and management of personnel, right methods of in-

struction and preparation of competent teachers, scientific adjustment of taxation, efficient management of funds, and so on. These are technical matters, as much so as the construction of an efficient engine for purposes of traction or locomotion. Like it they are to be settled by inquiry into facts; and as the inquiry can be carried on only by those especially equipped, so the results of inquiry can be utilized only by trained technicians. What has counting heads, decision by majority and the whole apparatus of traditional government to do with such things? Given such considerations, and the public and its organization for political ends is not only a ghost, but a ghost which walks and talks, and obscures, confuses and misleads governmental action in a disastrous way.

Personally I am far from thinking that such considerations, pertinent as they are to administrative activities, cover the entire political field. They ignore forces which have to be composed and resolved before technical and specialized action can come into play. But they aid in giving definiteness and point to a fundamental question: What, after all, is the public under present conditions? What are the reasons for its eclipse? What hinders it from finding and identifying itself? By what means shall its inchoate and amorphous estate be organized into effective political action relevant to present social needs and opportunities? What has happened to the Public in the century and a half since the theory of political democracy was urged with such assurance and hope?

Previous discussion has brought to light some conditions out of which the public is generated. It has also set forth some of the causes through which a "new age of human relationships" has been brought into being. These two arguments form the premises which, when they are related to each other, will provide our answer to the questions just raised. Indirect, extensive, enduring and serious consequences of conjoint and interacting behavior call a public into existence having a common interest in controlling these consequences. But the machine age has so enormously expanded, multiplied, intensified and complicated the scope of the indirect consequences, have formed such immense and consolidated unions in action, on an impersonal rather than a community basis, that the resultant public cannot identify and distinguish itself. And this discovery is obviously an antecedent condition of any effective organization on its part. Such is our thesis regarding the eclipse which the public idea and interest have undergone. There are too many publics and too much of public concern for our existing resources to cope with. The problem of a democratically organized public is primarily and essentially an intellectual problem, in a degree to which the political affairs of prior ages offer no parallel.

Our concern at this time is to state how it is that the machine age in developing the Great Society has invaded and partially disintegrated the small communities of former times without generating a Great Community. The facts are familiar enough; our especial affair is to point out their connections with the difficulties under which the organization of a democratic public is laboring. For the very familiarity with the phenomena conceals their significance and blinds us to their relation to immediate political problems.

The scope of the Great War furnishes an urgent as well as convenient starting point for the discussion. The extent of that war is unparalleled, because the conditions involved in it are so new. The dynastic conflicts of the seventeenth century are called by the same name: we have only one word, "war." The sameness of the word too easily conceals from us the difference in significance. We think of all wars as much the same thing, only the last one was horrible beyond others. Colonies were drawn in: self-governing ones entered voluntarily; possessions were levied upon for troops; alliances were formed with remote countries in spite of diversities of race and culture, as in the cases of Great Britain and Japan, Germany and Turkey. Literally every continent upon the globe was involved. Indirect effects were as broad as direct. Not merely soldiers, but finance, industry and opinion were mobilized and consolidated. Neutrality was a precarious affair. There was a critical epoch in the history of the world when the Roman Empire assembled in itself the lands and peoples of the Mediterranean basin. The World War stands out as an indubitable proof that what then happened for a region has now happened for the world, only there is now no comprehensive political organization to include the various divided yet interdependent countries. Any one who even partially visualizes the scene has a convincing reminder of the meaning of the Great Society: that it exists, and that it is not integrated.

Extensive, enduring, intricate and serious indirect consequences of the conjoint activity of a comparatively few persons traverse the globe. The similes of the stone cast into the pool, ninepins in a row, the spark which kindles a vast conflagration, are pale in comparison with the reality. The spread of the war seemed like the movement of an uncontrolled natural catastrophe. The consolidation of peoples in enclosed, nominally independent, national states has its counterpart in the fact that their acts affect groups and individuals in other states all over the world. The connections and ties which transferred energies set in motion in one spot to all parts of the earth were not tangible and visible; they do not stand out as do politically bounded states. But the war is there to show that they are as real, and to prove that they are not organized and regulated. It suggests that existing political and legal forms and arrangements are incompetent to deal with the situation. For the latter is the joint product of the existing constitution of the political state and the working of non-polit-

ical forces not adjusted to political forms. We cannot
expect the causes of a disease to combine effectually to
cure the disease they create. The need is that the non-
political forces organize themselves to transform existing political structures: that the divided and troubled
publics integrate.

In general, the non-political forces are the expressions of a technological age injected into an
inherited political scheme which operates to deflect
and distort their normal operation. The industrial
and commercial relations that created the situation
of which the war is a manifestation are as evident in
small things as great. They were exhibited, not only
in the struggle for raw materials, for distant markets,
and in staggering national debts, but in local and un-
important phenomena. Travelers finding themselves
away from home could not get their letters of credit
cashed even in countries not then at war. Stock-
markets closed on one hand, and profiteers piled up
their millions on the other. One instance may be cited
from domestic affairs. The plight of the farmer since
the war has created a domestic political issue. A great
demand was generated for food and other agricultural
products; prices rose. In addition to this economic
stimulus, farmers were objects of constant political
exhortation to increase their crops. Inflation and
temporary prosperity followed. The end of active
warfare came. Impoverished countries could not buy
and pay for foodstuffs up to even a pre-war level.

Taxes were enormously increased. Currencies were depreciated; the world's gold supply centered here. The stimulus of war and of national extravagance piled up the inventories of factories and merchants. Wages and the prices of agricultural implements increased. When deflation came it found a restricted market, increased costs of production, and farmers burdened with mortgages lightly assumed during the period of frenzied expansion.

This instance is not cited because it is peculiarly important in comparison with other consequences which have happened, especially in Europe. It is relatively insignificant by contrast with them, and in contrast with the arousal of nationalistic sentiments which has everywhere taken place since the war in so-called backward countries. But it shows the ramifying consequences of our intricate and interdependent economic relations, and it shows how little prevision and regulation exist. The farming population could hardly have acted with knowledge of the consequences of the fundamental relations in which they were implicated. They could make a momentary and improvised response to them, but they could not manage their affairs in controlled adaptation to the course of events. They present themselves as hapless subjects of overwhelming operations with which they were hardly acquainted and over which they had no more control than over the vicissitudes of climate.

The illustration cannot be objected to on the ground

that it rests upon the abnormal situation of war. The
war itself was a normal manifestation of the underlying
unintegrated state of society. The local face-to-face
community has been invaded by forces so vast, so
remote in initiation, so far-reaching in scope and so
complexly indirect in operation, that they are, from
the standpoint of the members of local social units,
unknown. Man, as has been often remarked, has difficulty in getting on either with or without his fellows,
even in neighborhoods. He is not more successful in
getting on with them when they act at a great distance
in ways invisible to him. An inchoate public is capable
of organization only when indirect consequences are
perceived, and when it is possible to project agencies
which order their occurrence. At present, many consequences are felt rather than perceived; they are
suffered, but they cannot be said to be known, for they
are not, by those who experience them, referred to their
origins. It goes, then, without saying that agencies
are not established which canalize the streams of
social action and thereby regulate them. Hence the
publics are amorphous and unarticulated.

There was a time when a man might entertain a few
general political principles and apply them with some
confidence. A citizen believed in states' rights or in a
centralized federal government; in free trade or protection. It did not involve much mental strain to
imagine that by throwing in his lot with one party
or another he could so express his views that his belief

would count in government. For the average voter
to-day the tariff question is a complicated medley of
infinite detail, schedules of rates specific and *ad valorem*
on countless things, many of which he does not recognize by name, and with respect to which he can form
no judgment. Probably not one voter in a thousand
even reads the scores of pages in which the rates of
toll are enumerated and he would not be much wiser if
he did. The average man gives it up as a bad job.
At election time, appeal to some time-worn slogan may
galvanize him into a temporary notion that he has con-
victions on an important subject, but except for manufacturers and dealers who have some interest at stake in
this or that schedule, belief lacks the qualities which
attach to beliefs about matters of personal concern.
Industry is too complex and intricate.

Again the voter may by personal predilection or
inherited belief incline towards magnifying the scope of
local governments and inveigh against the evils of centralization. But he is vehemently sure of social
evils attending the liquor traffic. He finds that the
prohibitory law of his locality, township, county or
state, is largely nullified by the importation of liquor
from outside, made easy by modern means of transportation. So he becomes an advocate of a national
amendment giving the central government power to
regulate the manufacture and sale of intoxicating
drinks. This brings in its train a necessary extension
of federal officials and powers. Thus to-day, the south,

the traditional home of the states' rights doctrine, is the chief supporter of national prohibition and Volstead Act. It would not be possible to say how many voters have thought of the relation between their professed general principle and their special position on the liquor question: probably not many. On the other hand, life-long Hamiltonians, proclaimers of the dangers of particularistic local autonomy, are opposed to prohibition. Hence they play a tune *ad hoc* on the Jeffersonian flute. Gibes at inconsistency are, however, as irrelevant as they are easy. The social situation has been so changed by the factors of an industrial age that traditional general principles have little practical meaning. They persist as emotional cries rather than as reasoned ideas.

The same criss-crossing occurs with reference to regulation of railways. The opponent of a strong federal government finds, being a farmer or shipper, that rates are too high; he also finds that railways pay little attention to state boundaries, that lines once local are parts of vast systems and that state legislation and administration are ineffectual for his purpose. He calls for national regulation. Some partisan of the powers of the central government, on the other hand, being an investor in stocks and bonds, finds that his income is likely to be unfavorably affected by federal action and he promptly protests against the vexatious tendency to appeal to national aid, which has now become in his eyes a foolish paternalism. The developments of industry and commerce have so complicated affairs that a clear-cut, generally applicable, standard of judgment becomes practically impossible. The forest cannot be seen for the trees nor the trees for the forest.

A striking example of the shift of the actual tenor of doctrines—that is, of their consequences in application—is presented in the history of the doctrine of Individualism, interpreted to signify a minimum of governmental "interference" with industry and trade. At the outset, it was held by "progressives," by those who were protesting against the inherited régime of rules of law and administration. Vested interests, on the contrary, were mainly in favor of the old status. To-day the industrial-property régime being established, the doctrine is the intellectual bulwark of the standpatter and reactionary. He it is that now wants to be let alone, and who utters the war-cry of liberty for private industry, thrift, contract and their pecuniary fruit. In the United States the name "liberal," as a party designation, is still employed to designate a progressive in political matters. In most other countries, the "liberal" party is that which represents established and vested commercial and financial interests in protest against governmental regulation. The irony of history is nowhere more evident than in the reversal of the practical meaning of the term "liberalism" in spite of a literal continuity of theory.

Political apathy, which is a natural product of the discrepancies between actual practices and traditional

machinery, ensues from inability to identify one's self
with definite issues.   These are hard to find and locate
in the vast complexities of current life.   When traditional war-cries have lost their import in practical
policies which are consonant with them, they are
readily dismissed as bunk.   Only habit and tradition,
rather than reasoned conviction, together with a vague
faith in doing one's civic duty, send to the polls a
considerable percentage of the fifty per cent. who still
vote.   And of them it is a common remark that a large
number vote against something or somebody rather
than for anything or anybody, except when powerful
agencies create a scare.   The old principles do not
fit contemporary life as it is lived, however well they
may have expressed the vital interests of the times in
which they arose.   Thousands feel their hollowness
even if they cannot make their feeling articulate.   The
confusion which has resulted from the size and ram-
ifications of social activities has rendered men skep-
tical of the efficiency of political action.   Who is sufficient unto these things?   Men feel that they are
caught in the sweep of forces too vast to understand
or master.   Thought is brought to a standstill and
action paralyzed.   Even the specialist finds it difficult
to trace the chain of "cause and effect"; and even he
operates only after the event, looking backward, while
meantime social activities have moved on to effect a
new state of affairs.

Similar   considerations   account   for   depreciation

of the machinery of democratic political action in contrast with a rising appreciation of the need of expert administrators. For example, one of the by-products of the war was the investment of the government at Muscle Shoals for the manufacture of nitrogen, a chemical product of great importance to the farmer, as well as to armies in the field. The disposition and utilization of the plant have become matters of political dispute. The questions involved, questions of science, agriculture, industry and finance, are highly technical. How many voters are competent to measure all the factors involved in arriving at a decision? And if they were competent after studying it, how many have the time to devote to it? It is true that this matter does not come before the electorate directly, but the technical difficulty of the problem is reflected in the confused paralysis of the legislators whose business it is to deal with it. The confused situation is further complicated by the invention of other and cheaper methods of producing nitrates. Again, the rapid development of hydro-electric and super-power is a matter of public concern. In the long run, few questions exceed it in importance. Aside from business corporations which have a direct interest in it and some engineers, how many citizens have the data or the ability to secure and estimate the facts involved in its settlement? One further illustration: Two things which intimately concern a local public are street-railway transportation and the marketing of food products. But the history

of municipal politics shows in most cases a flare-up of
intense interest followed by a period of indifference.
Results come home to the masses of the people. But
the very size, heterogeneity and nobility of urban populations, the vast capital required, the technical character of the engineering problems involved, soon tire the
attention of the average voter. I think the three instances are fairly typical. The ramification of the
issues before the public is so wide and intricate, the
technical matters involved are so specialized, the de-
tails are so many and so shifting, that the public cannot for any length of time identify and hold itself.
It is not that there is no public, no large body of
persons having a common interest in the consequences
of social transactions. There is too much public, a
public too diffused and scattered and too intricate in
composition. And there are too many publics, for conjoint actions which have indirect, serious and enduring
consequences are multitudinous beyond comparison,
and each one of them crosses the others and generates
its own group of persons especially affected with little
to hold these different publics together in an integrated
whole.

The picture is not complete without taking into account the many competitors with effective political interest. Political concerns have, of course, always had
strong rivals. Persons have always been, for the most
part, taken up with their more immediate work and
play. The power of "bread and the circus" to divert

attention from public matters is an old story. But
now the industrial conditions which have enlarged,
complicated and multiplied public interests have also
multiplied and intensified formidable rivals to them.
In countries where political life has been most successfully conducted in the past, there was a class
specially set aside, as it were, who made political affairs
their special business. Aristotle could not conceive
a body of citizens competent to carry on politics consisting of others than those who had leisure, that is,
of those who were relieved from all other preoccupa-
tions, especially that of making a livelihood. Political
life, till recent times, bore out his belief. Those who
took an active part in politics were "gentlemen," persons who had had property and money long enough,
and enough of it, so that its further pursuit was vulgar and beneath their station. To-day, so great and
powerful is the sweep of the industrial current, the
person of leisure is usually an idle person. Persons
have their own business to attend to, and "business"
has its own precise and specialized meaning. Politics
thus tends to become just another "business": the especial concern of bosses and the managers of the
machine.

The increase in the number, variety and cheapness of
amusements represents a powerful diversion from
political concern. The members of an inchoate public
have too many ways of enjoyment, as well as of work,
to give much thought to organization into an effective

public. Man is a consuming and sportive animal as
well as a political one. What is significant is that
access to means of amusement has been rendered easy
and cheap beyond anything known in the past. The
present era of "prosperity" may not be enduring. But
the movie, radio, cheap reading matter and motor car
with all they stand for have come to stay. That
they did not originate in deliberate desire to divert
attention from political interests does not lessen their
effectiveness in that direction. The political elements
in the constitution of the human being, those having
to do with citizenship, are crowded to one side. In
most circles it is hard work to sustain conversation
on a political theme; and once initiated, it is quickly
dismissed with a yawn. Let there be introduced the
topic of the mechanism and accomplishment of various
makes of motor cars or the respective merits of ac-
tresses, and the dialogue goes on at a lively pace. The
thing to be remembered is that this cheapened and
multiplied access to amusement is the product of the
machine age, intensified by the business tradition which
causes provision of means for an enjoyable passing of
time to be one of the most profitable of occupations.

One phase of the workings of a technological age,
with its unprecedented command of natural energies,
while it is implied in what has been said, needs explicit
attention. The older publics, in being local communities, largely homogeneous with one another, were also,
as the phrase goes, static. They changed, of course,

but barring war, catastrophe and great migrations, the modifications were gradual. They proceeded slowly and were largely unperceived by those undergoing them. The newer forces have created mobile and fluctuating associational forms. The common complaints of the disintegration of family life may be placed in evidence. The movement from rural to urban assemblies is also the result and proof of this mobility. Nothing stays long put, not even the associations by which business and industry are carried on. The mania for motion and speed is a symptom of the restless instability of social life, and it operates to intensify the causes from which it springs. Steel replaces wood and masonry for buildings; ferro-concrete modifies steel, and some invention may work a further revolution. Muscle Shoals was acquired to produce nitrogen, and new methods have already made antiquated the supposed need of great accumulation of water power. Any selected illustration suffers because of the heterogeneous mass of cases to select from. How can a public be organized, we may ask, when literally it does not stay in place? Only deep issues or those which can be made to appear such can find a common denominator among all the shifting and unstable relationships. Attachment is a very different function of life from affection. Affections will continue as long as the heart beats. But attachment requires something more than organic causes. The very things which stimulate and intensify affections may

undermine attachments. For these are bred in tranquil
stability; they are nourished in constant relationships.
Acceleration of mobility disturbs them at their root.
And without abiding attachments associations are too
shifting and shaken to permit a public readily to locate
and identify itself.

The new era of human relationships in which we
live is one marked by mass production for remote markets, by cable and telephone, by cheap printing, by
railway and steam navigation. Only geographically
did Columbus discover a new world. The actual new
world has been generated in the last hundred years.
Steam and electricity have done more to alter the conditions under which men associate together than all
the agencies which affected human relationships before
our time. There are those who lay the blame for all
the evils of our lives on steam, electricity and machinery. It is always convenient to have a devil as well as a
savior to bear the responsibilities of humanity. In
reality, the trouble springs rather from the ideas and
absence of ideas in connection with which technological
factors operate. Mental and moral beliefs and ideals
change more slowly than outward conditions. If the
ideals associated with the higher life of our cultural
past have been impaired, the fault is primarily with
them. Ideals and standards formed without regard
to the means by which they are to be achieved and incarnated in flesh are bound to be thin and wavering.
Since the aims, desires and purposes created by a

machine age do not connect with tradition, there are two sets of rival ideals, and those which have actual instrumentalities at their disposal have the advantage. Because the two are rivals and because the older ones retain their glamor and sentimental prestige in literature and religion, the newer ones are perforce harsh and narrow. For the older symbols of ideal life still engage thought and command loyalty. Conditions have changed, but every aspect of life, from religion and education to property and trade, shows that nothing approaching a transformation has taken place in ideas and ideals. Symbols control sentiment and thought, and the new age has no symbols consonant with its activities. Intellectual instrumentalities for the formation of an organized public are more inadequate than its overt means. The ties which hold men together in action are numerous, tough and subtle. But they are invisible and intangible. We have the physical tools of communication as never before. The thoughts and aspirations congruous with them are not communicated, and hence are not common. Without such communication the public will remain shadowy and formless, seeking spasmodically for itself, but seizing and holding its shadow rather than its substance. Till the Great Society is converted into a Great Community, the Public will remain in eclipse. Communication can alone create a great community. Our Babel is not one of tongues but of the signs and symbols without which shared experience is impossible.

CHAPTER V

SEARCH FOR THE GREAT COMMUNITY

We have had occasion to refer in passing to the distinction between democracy as a social idea and political democracy as a system of government. The two are, of course, connected. The idea remains barren and empty save as it is incarnated in human relationships. Yet in discussion they must be distinguished. The idea of democracy is a wider and fuller idea than can be exemplified in the state even at its best. To be realized it must affect all modes of human association, the family, the school, industry, religion. And even as far as political arrangements are concerned, governmental institutions are but a mechanism for securing to an idea channels of effective operation. It will hardly do to say that criticisms of the political machinery leave the believer in the idea untouched. For, as far as they are justified—and no candid believer can deny that many of them are only too well grounded— they arouse him to bestir himself in order that the idea may find a more adequate machinery through which to work. What the faithful insist upon, however, is that the idea and its external organs and structures are not to be identified. We object to the common supposition of the foes of existing democratic government

143

that the accusations against it touch the social and moral aspirations and ideas which underlie the political forms. The old saying that the cure for the ills of democracy is more democracy is not apt if it means that the evils may be remedied by introducing more machinery of the same kind as that which already exists, or by refining and perfecting that machinery. But the phrase may also indicate the need of returning to the idea itself, of clarifying and deepening our apprehension of it, and of employing our sense of its meaning to criticize and re-make its political manifestations.

Confining ourselves, for the moment, to political democracy, we must, in any case, renew our protest against the assumption that the idea has itself produced the governmental practices which obtain in democratic states: General suffrage, elected representatives, majority rule, and so on. The idea has influenced the concrete political movement, but it has not caused it. The transition from family and dynastic government supported by the loyalties of tradition to popular government was the outcome primarily of technological discoveries and inventions working a change in the customs by which men had been bound together. It was not due to the doctrines of doctrinaires. The forms to which we are accustomed in democratic governments represent the cumulative effect of a multitude of events, unpremeditated as far as political effects were concerned and having unpredictable consequences. There is no sanctity in universal suffrage, frequent elections, majority rule, congressional and cabinet government. These things are devices evolved in the direction in which the current was moving, each wave of which involved at the time of its impulsion a minimum of departure from antecedent custom and law. The devices served a purpose; but the purpose was rather that of meeting existing needs which had become too intense to be ignored, than that of forwarding the democratic idea. In spite of all defects, they served their own purpose well.

Looking back, with the aid which *ex posto facto* experience can give, it would be hard for the wisest to devise schemes which, under the circumstances, would have met the needs better. In this retrospective glance, it is possible, however, to see how the doctrinal formulations which accompanied them were inadequate, one-sided and positively erroneous. In fact they were hardly more than political war-cries adopted to help in carrying on some immediate agitation or in justifying some particular practical polity struggling for recognition, even though they were asserted to be absolute truths of human nature or of morals. The doctrines served a particular local pragmatic need. But often their very adaptation to immediate circumstances unfitted them, pragmatically, to meet more enduring and more extensive needs. They lived to cumber the political ground, obstructing progress, all the more so because they were uttered and held not as hypotheses with which to direct social experimentation but as final truths, dogmas. No wonder they call urgently for revision and displacement.

Nevertheless the current has set steadily in one direction: toward democratic forms. That government exists to serve its community, and that this purpose cannot be achieved unless the community itself shares in selecting its governors and determining their policies, are a deposit of fact left, as far as we can see, permanently in the wake of doctrines and forms, however transitory the latter. They are not the whole of the democratic idea, but they express it in its political phase. Belief in this political aspect is not a mystic faith as if in some overruling providence that cares for children, drunkards and others unable to help themselves. It marks a well-attested conclusion from historic facts. We have every reason to think that whatever changes may take place in existing democratic machinery, they will be of a sort to make the interest of the public a more supreme guide and criterion of governmental activity, and to enable the public to form and manifest its purposes still more authoritatively. In this sense the cure for the ailments of democracy is more democracy. The prime difficulty, as we have seen, is that of discovering the means by which a scattered, mobile and manifold public may so recognize itself as to define and express its interests. This discovery is necessarily precedent to any fundamental change in the machinery. We are not concerned therefore to set forth counsels as to advisable improvements in the political forms of democracy. Many have been suggested. It is no derogation of their relative worth to say that consideration of these changes is not at present an affair of primary importance. The problem lies deeper; it is in the first instance an intellectual problem: the search for conditions under which the Great Society may become the Great Community. When these conditions are brought into being they will make their own forms. Until they have come about, it is somewhat futile to consider what political machinery will suit them.

In a search for the conditions under which the inchoate public now extant may function democratically, we may proceed from a statement of the nature of the democratic idea in its generic social sense.[1] From the standpoint of the individual, it consists in having a responsible share according to capacity in forming and directing the activities of the groups to which one belongs and in participating according to need in the values which the groups sustain. From the standpoint of the groups, it demands liberation of the potentialities of members of a group in harmony with the interests and goods which are common. Since every individual is a member of many groups, this specification cannot be fulfilled except when different groups interact flexibly and fully in connection with other groups. A member

[1] The most adequate discussion of this ideal with which I am acquainted is T. V. Smith's "The Democratic Way of Life."

of a robber band may express his powers in a way consonant with belonging to that group and be directed
by the interest common to its members.   But he does
so only at the cost of repression of those of his potentialities which can be realized only through membership
in other groups.   The robber band cannot interact
flexibly with other groups; it can act only through
isolating itself.   It must prevent the operation of all
interests save those which circumscribe it in its separateness.   But a good citizen finds his conduct as a
member of a political group enriching and enriched
by his participation in family life, industry, scientific
and artistic associations.   There is a free give-and-
take: fullness of integrated personality is therefore possible of achievement, since the pulls and responses of
different groups reënforce one another and their values
accord.

Regarded as an idea, democracy is not an alternative to other principles of associated life.   It is the idea
of community life itself.   It is an ideal in the only intelligible sense of an ideal: namely, the tendency and
movement of some thing which exists carried to its
final limit, viewed as completed, perfected.   Since
things do not attain such fulfillment but are in actuality distracted and interfered with, democracy in this
sense is not a fact and never will be.   But neither in
this sense is there or has there ever been anything which
is a community in its full measure, a community un-
alloyed by alien elements.   The idea or ideal of a com-

munity presents, however, actual phases of associated life as they are freed from restrictive and disturbing elements, and are contemplated as having attained their limit of development. Wherever there is conjoint activity whose consequences are appreciated as good by all singular persons who take part in it, and where the realization of the good is such as to effect an energetic desire and effort to sustain it in being just because it is a good shared by all, there is in so far a community. The clear consciousness of a communal life, in all its implications, constitutes the idea of democracy.

Only when we start from a community as a fact, grasp the fact in thought so as to clarify and enhance its constituent elements, can we reach an idea of democracy which is not utopian. The conceptions and shibboleths which are traditionally associated with the idea of democracy take on a veridical and directive meaning only when they are construed as marks and traits of an association which realizes the defining characteristics of a community. Fraternity, liberty and equality isolated from communal life are hopeless abstractions. Their separate assertion leads to mushy sentimentalism or else to extravagant and fanatical violence which in the end defeats its own aims. Equality then becomes a creed of mechanical identity which is false to facts and impossible of realization. Effort to attain it is divisive of the vital bonds which hold men together; as far as it puts forth issue, the outcome

is a mediocrity in which good is common only in the
sense of being average and vulgar. Liberty is then
thought of as independence of social ties, and ends in
dissolution and anarchy. It is more difficult to sever
the idea of brotherhood from that of a community,
and hence it is either practically ignored in the movements which identify democracy with Individualism,
or else it is a sentimentally appended tag. In its just
connection with communal experience, fraternity is
another name for the consciously appreciated goods
which accrue from an association in which all share, and
which give direction to the conduct of each. Liberty
is that secure release and fulfillment of personal potentialities which take place only in rich and manifold
association with others: the power to be an individual-
ized self making a distinctive contribution and enjoy-
ing in its own way the fruits of association. Equality
denotes the unhampered share which each individual
member of the community has in the consequences of
associated action. It is equitable because it is measured
only by need and capacity to utilize, not by extraneous
factors which deprive one in order that another may
take and have. A baby in the family is equal with
others, not because of some antecedent and structural
quality which is the same as that of others, but in so
far as his needs for care and development are attended
to without being sacrificed to the superior strength,
possessions and matured abilities of others. Equality
does not signify that kind of mathematical or physical

equivalence in virtue of which any one element may be substituted for another. It denotes effective regard for whatever is distinctive and unique in each, irrespective of physical and psychological inequalities. It is not a natural possession but is a fruit of the community when its action is directed by its character as a community.

Associated or joint activity is a condition of the creation of a community. But association itself is physical and organic, while communal life is moral, that is emotionally, intellectually, consciously sustained. Human beings combine in behavior as directly and unconsciously as do atoms, stellar masses and cells; as directly and unknowingly as they divide and repel. They do so in virtue of their own structure, as man and woman unite, as the baby seeks the breast and the breast is there to supply its need. They do so from external circumstances, pressure from without, as atoms combine or separate in presence of an electric charge, or as sheep huddle together from the cold. Associated activity needs no explanation; things are made that way. But no amount of aggregated collective action of itself constitutes a community. For beings who observe and think, and whose ideas are absorbed by impulses and become sentiments and interests, "we" is as inevitable as "I." But "we" and "our" exist only when the consequences of combined action are perceived and become an object of desire and effort, just as "I" and "mine" appear on the scene only when a distinctive share in mutual action is consciously asserted or claimed. Human associations may be ever so organic in origin and firm in operation, but they develop into societies in a human sense only as their consequences, being known, are esteemed and sought for. Even if "society" were as much an organism as some writers have held, it would not on that account be society. Interactions, transactions, occur *de facto* and the results of interdependence follow. But participation in activities and sharing in results are additive concerns. They demand *communication* as a prerequisite.

Combined activity happens among human beings; but when nothing else happens it passes as inevitably into some other mode of interconnected activity as does the interplay of iron and the oxygen of water. What takes place is wholly describable in terms of energy, or, as we say in the case of human interactions, of force. Only when there exist *signs* or *symbols* of activities and of their outcome can the flux be viewed as from without, be arrested for consideration and esteem, and be regulated. Lightning strikes and rives a tree or rock, and the resulting fragments take up and continue the process of interaction, and so on and on. But when phases of the process are represented by signs, a new medium is interposed. As symbols are related to one another, the important relations of a course of events are recorded and are preserved as meanings. Recollection and foresight are possible; the

new medium facilitates calculation, planning, and a
new kind of action which intervenes in what happens
to direct its course in the interest of what is foreseen
and desired.

Symbols in turn depend upon and promote communication. The results of conjoint experience
are considered and transmitted. Events cannot be
passed from one to another, but meanings may be
shared by means of signs. Wants and impulses are then
attached to common meanings. They are thereby transformed into desires and purposes, which, since they
implicate a common or mutually understood meaning,
present new ties, converting a conjoint activity into a
community of interest and endeavor. Thus there is
generated what, metaphorically, may be termed a general will and social consciousness: desire and choice on
the part of individuals in behalf of activities that,
by means of symbols, are communicable and shared
by all concerned. A community thus presents an
order of energies transmuted into one of meanings
which are appreciated and mutually referred by each
to every other on the part of those engaged in combined action. "Force" is not eliminated but is transformed in use and direction by ideas and sentiments
made possible by means of symbols.

The work of conversion of the physical and organic
phase of associated behavior into a community of
action saturated and regulated by mutual interest in
shared meanings, consequences which are translated

into ideas and desired objects by means of symbols, does not occur all at once nor completely. At any given time, it sets a problem rather than marks a settled achievement. We are born organic beings associated with others, but we are not born members of a community. The young have to be brought within the traditions, outlook and interests which characterize a community by means of education: by unremitting instruction and by learning in connection with the phenomena of overt association. Everything which is distinctively human is learned, not native, even though it could not be learned without native structures which mark man off from other animals. To learn in a human way and to human effect is not just to acquire added skill through refinement of original capacities.

To learn to be human is to develop through the give-and-take of communication an effective sense of being an individually distinctive member of a community; one who understands and appreciates its beliefs, desires and methods, and who contributes to a further conversion of organic powers into human resources and values. But this translation is never finished. The old Adam, the unregenerate element in human nature, persists. It shows itself wherever the method obtains of attaining results by use of force instead of by the method of communication and enlightenment. It manifests itself more subtly, pervasively and effectually when knowledge and the instrumentalities of skill which

are the product of communal life are employed in the
service of wants and impulses which have not themselves
been modified by reference to a shared interest. To the
doctrine of "natural" economy which held that commercial exchange would bring about such an interdependence that harmony would automatically result, Rousseau gave an adequate answer in advance. He pointed
out that interdependence provides just the situation
which makes it possible and worth while for the stronger
and abler to exploit others for their own ends, to keep
others in a state of subjection where they can be utilized
as animated tools. The remedy he suggested, a return
to a condition of independence based on isolation, was
hardly seriously meant. But its desperateness is evidence of the urgency of the problem. Its negative
character was equivalent to surrender of any hope
of solution. By contrast it indicates the nature of the
only possible solution: the perfecting of the means
and ways of communication of meanings so that genuinely shared interest in the consequences of interdependent activities may inform desire and effort and
thereby direct action.

This is the meaning of the statement that the problem is a moral one dependent upon intelligence and education. We have in our prior account sufficiently emphasized the rôle of technological and industrial factors in creating the Great Society. What was said may
even have seemed to imply acceptance of the determin-
istic version of an economic interpretation of history

and institutions. It is silly and futile to ignore and deny
economic facts. They do not cease to operate because
we refuse to note them, or because we smear them over
with sentimental idealizations. As we have also noted,
they generate as their result overt and external conditions of action and these are known with various degrees
of adequacy. What actually happens in consequence
of industrial forces is dependent upon the presence
or absence of perception and communication of consequences, upon foresight and its effect upon desire and
endeavor. Economic agencies produce one result when
they are left to work themselves out on the merely
physical level, or on that level modified only as the knowledge, skill and technique which the community has
accumulated are transmitted to its members unequally
and by chance. They have a different outcome in the
degree in which knowledge of consequences is equitably
distributed, and action is animated by an informed
and lively sense of a shared interest. The doctrine of
economic interpretation as usually stated ignores the
transformation which meanings may effect; it passes
over the new medium which communication may inter-
pose between industry and its eventual consequences.
It is obsessed by the illusion which vitiated the
"natural economy": an illusion due to failure to note
the difference made in action by perception and publication of its consequences, actual and possible. It
thinks in terms of antecedents, not of the eventual; of
origins, not fruits.

We have returned, through this apparent excursion, to the question in which our earlier discussion culminated: What are the conditions under which it is possible for the Great Society to approach more closely and vitally the status of a Great Community, and thus take form in genuinely democratic societies and state? What are the conditions under which we may reasonably picture the Public emerging from its eclipse?

The study will be an intellectual or hypothetical one. There will be no attempt to state how the required conditions might come into existence, nor to prophesy that they will occur. The object of the analysis will be to show that *unless* ascertained specifications are realized, the Community cannot be organized as a democratically effective Public. It is not claimed that the conditions which will be noted will suffice, but only that at least they are indispensable. In other words, we shall endeavor to frame a hypothesis regarding the democratic state to stand in contrast with the earlier doctrine which has been nullified by the course of events.

Two essential constituents in that older theory, as will be recalled, were the notions that each individual is of himself equipped with the intelligence needed, under the operation of self-interest, to engage in political affairs; and that general suffrage, frequent elections of officials and majority rule are sufficient to ensure the responsibility of elected rulers to the desires and interests of the public. As we shall see, the second conception is logically bound up with the first and stands

or falls with it.   At the basis of the scheme lies what
Lippmann has well called the idea of the "omni-
competent" individual: competent to frame policies, to
judge their results; competent to know in all situations
demanding political action what is for his own good,
and competent to enforce his idea of good and the
will to effect it against contrary forces.   Subsequent
history has proved that the assumption involved illusion.   Had it not been for the misleading influence of a
false psychology, the illusion might have been detected
in advance.   But current philosophy held that ideas
and knowledge were functions of a mind or consciousness which originated in individuals by means of
isolated contact with objects.   But in fact, knowledge is
a function of association and communication; it depends upon tradition, upon tools and methods socially
transmitted, developed and sanctioned.   Faculties of ef-
fectual observation, reflection and desire are habits acquired under the influence of the culture and institutions of society, not ready-made inherent powers.
The fact that man acts from crudely intelligized emotion and from habit rather than from rational consideration, is now so familiar that it is not easy to
appreciate that the other idea was taken seriously as
the basis of economic and political philosophy.   The
measure of truth which it contains was derived from
observation of a relatively small group of shrewd business men who regulated their enterprises by calculation
and accounting, and of citizens of small and stable

local communities who were so intimately acquainted
with the persons and affairs of their locality that they
could pass competent judgment upon the bearing of
proposed measures upon their own concerns.

Habit is the mainspring of human action, and habits
are formed for the most part under the influence of the
customs of a group. The organic structure of man
entails the formation of habit, for, whether we wish
it or not, whether we are aware of it or not, every
act effects a modification of attitude and set which
directs future behavior. The dependence of habit-
forming upon those habits of a group which constitute
customs and institutions is a natural consequence of
the helplessness of infancy. The social consequences of
habit have been stated once for all by James: "Habit is
the enormous fly-wheel of society, its most precious con-
servative influence. It alone is what keeps us within
the bounds of ordinance, and saves the children of
fortune from the uprisings of the poor. It alone pre-
vents the hardest and most repulsive walks of life from
being deserted by those brought up to tread therein.
It keeps the fisherman and the deck-hand at sea through
the winter; it holds the miner in his darkness, and
nails the country-man to his log cabin and his lonely
farm through all the months of snow; it protects us
from invasion by the natives of the desert and the
frozen zone. It dooms us all to fight out the battle
of life upon the lines of our nurture or our early choice,
and to make the best of a pursuit that disagrees, be-

cause there is no other for which we are fitted and it
is too late to begin again.   It keeps different social
strata from mixing."

The influence of habit is decisive because all distinctively human action has to be learned, and the
very heart, blood and sinews of learning is creation of
habitudes.   Habits bind us to orderly and established
ways of action because they generate ease, skill and
interest in things to which we have grown used and because they instigate fear to walk in different ways, and
because they leave us incapacitated for the trial of
them.   Habit does not preclude the use of thought, but
it determines the channels within which it operates.
Thinking is secreted in the interstices of habits.   The
sailor, miner, fisherman and farmer think, but their
thoughts fall within the framework of accustomed occupations and relationships.   We dream beyond the
limits of use and wont, but only rarely does revery become a source of acts which break bounds; so rarely
that we name those in whom it happens demonic
geniuses and marvel at the spectacle.   Thinking itself
becomes habitual along certain lines; a specialized occu-
pation.   Scientific men, philosophers, literary persons,
are not men and women who have so broken the bonds
of habits that pure reason and emotion undefiled by use
and wont speak through them.   They are persons of a
specialized infrequent habit.   Hence the idea that men
are moved by an intelligent and calculated regard for
their own good is pure mythology.   Even if the prin-

ciple of self-love actuated behavior, it would still be
true that the *objects* in which men find their love manifested, the objects which they take as constituting their
peculiar interests, are set by habits reflecting social
customs.

These facts explain why the social doctrinaires of
the new industrial movement had so little prescience
of what was to follow in consequence of it. These facts
explain why the more things changed, the more they
were the same; they account, that is, for the fact that
instead of the sweeping revolution which was expected
to result from democratic political machinery, there
was in the main but a transfer of vested power from
one class to another. A few men, whether or not they
were good judges of their own true interest and good,
were competent judges of the conduct of business for
pecuniary profit, and of how the new governmental
machinery could be made to serve their ends. It would
have taken a new race of human beings to escape, in
the use made of political forms, from the influence of
deeply engrained habits, of old institutions and customary social status, with their inwrought limitations
of expectation, desire and demand. And such a race,
unless of disembodied angelic constitution, would simply
have taken up the task where human beings assumed
it upon emergence from the condition of anthropoid
apes. In spite of sudden and catastrophic revolutions,
the essential continuity of history is doubly guaranteed. Not only are personal desire and belief func-

tions of habit and custom, but the objective conditions which provide the resources and tools of action, together with its limitations, obstructions and traps, are precipitates of the past, perpetuating, willy-nilly, its hold and power. The creation of a *tabula rasa* in order to permit the creation of a new order is so impossible as to set at naught both the hope of buoyant revolutionaries and the timidity of scared conservatives.

Nevertheless, changes take place and are cumulative in character. Observation of them in the light of their recognized consequences arouses reflection, discovery, invention, experimentation. When a certain state of accumulated knowledge, of techniques and instrumentalities is attained, the process of change is so accelerated, that, as to-day, it appears externally to be the dominant trait. But there is a marked lag in any corresponding change of ideas and desires. Habits of opinion are the toughest of all habits; when they have become second nature, and are supposedly thrown out of the door, they creep in again as stealthily and surely as does first nature. And as they are modified, the alteration first shows itself negatively, in the disintegration of old beliefs, to be replaced by floating, volatile and accidentally snatched up opinions. Of course there has been an enormous increase in the amount of knowledge possessed by mankind, but it does not equal, probably, the increase in the amount of errors and half-truths which have got into circulation. In social and human matters, especially, the development of a critical sense and methods of discriminating judgment has not kept pace with the growth of careless reports and of motives for positive misrepresentation.

What is more important, however, is that so much of knowledge is not knowledge in the ordinary sense of the word, but is "science." The quotation marks are not used disrespectfully, but to suggest the technical character of scientific material. The layman takes certain conclusions which get into circulation to be science. But the scientific inquirer knows that they constitute science only in connection with the methods by which they are reached. Even when true, they are not science in virtue of their correctness, but by reason of the apparatus which is employed in reaching them. This apparatus is so highly specialized that it requires more labor to acquire ability to use and understand it than to get skill in any other instrumentalities possessed by man. Science, in other words, is a highly specialized language, more difficult to learn than any natural language. It is an artificial language, not in the sense of being factitious, but in that of being a work of intricate art, devoted to a particular purpose and not capable of being acquired nor understood in the way in which the mother tongue is learned. It is, indeed, conceivable that sometime methods of instruction will be devised which will enable laymen to read and hear scientific material with comprehension, even when they do not themselves use the apparatus which is science. The latter may then become for large numbers what students of language call a passive, if not an active, vocabulary. But that time is in the future.

For most men, save the scientific workers, science is a mystery in the hands of initiates, who have become adepts in virtue of following ritualistic ceremonies from which the profane herd is excluded. They are fortunate who get as far as a sympathetic appreciation of the methods which give pattern to the complicated apparatus: methods of analytic, experimental observation, mathematical formulation and deduction, constant and elaborate check and test. For most persons, the reality of the apparatus is found only in its embodiments in practical affairs, in mechanical devices and in techniques which touch life as it is lived. For them, electricity is *known* by means of the telephones, bells and lights they use, by the generators and magnetos in the automobiles they drive, by the trolley cars in which they ride. The physiology and biology they are acquainted with is that they have learned in taking precautions against germs and from the physicians they depend upon for health. The science of what might be supposed to be closest to them, of human nature, was for them an esoteric mystery until it was applied in advertising, salesmanship and personnel selection and management, and until, through psychiatry, it spilled over into life and popular consciousness, through its bearings upon "nerves," the morbidities and common forms of crankiness which make it difficult for persons to get along with one another and with themselves. Even now, popular psychology is a mass of cant, of slush and of superstition worthy of the most flourishing days of the medicine man.

Meanwhile the technological application of the complex apparatus which is science has revolutionized the conditions under which associated life goes on. This may be known as a fact which is stated in a proposition and assented to. But it is not known in the sense that men understand it. They do not know it as they know some machine which they operate, or as they know electric light and steam locomotives. They do not understand *how* the change has gone on nor *how* it affects their conduct. Not understanding its "how," they cannot use and control its manifestations. They undergo the consequences, they are affected by them. They cannot manage them, though some are fortunate enough—what is commonly called good fortune—to be able to exploit some phase of the process for their own personal profit. But even the most shrewd and successful man does not in any analytic and systematic way—in a way worthy to compare with the knowledge which he has won in lesser affairs by means of the stress of experience—know the system within which he operates. Skill and ability work within a framework which we have not created and do not comprehend. Some occupy strategic positions which give them advance information of forces that affect the market; and by training and an innate turn that way they have acquired a special technique which enables them to use the vast impersonal tide to turn their own wheels. They can dam the current here and release it there. The current itself is as much beyond them as was ever the river by the side of which some ingenious mechanic, employing a knowledge which was transmitted to him, erected his saw-mill to make boards of trees which he had not grown. That within limits those successful in affairs have knowledge and skill is not to be doubted. But such knowledge goes relatively but little further than that of the competent skilled operator who manages a machine. It suffices to employ the conditions which are before him. Skill enables him to turn the flux of events this way or that in his own neighborhood. It gives him no control of the flux.

Why should the public and its officers, even if the latter are termed statesmen, be wiser and more effective? The prime condition of a democratically organized public is a kind of knowledge and insight which does not yet exist. In its absence, it would be the height of absurdity to try to tell what it would be like if it existed. But some of the conditions which must be fulfilled if it is to exist can be indicated. We can borrow that much from the spirit and method of science even if we are ignorant of it as a specialized apparatus. An obvious requirement is freedom of social inquiry and of distribution of its conclusions.

The notion that men may be free in their thought even when they are not in its expression and dissemination has been sedulously propagated. It had its origin in the idea of a mind complete in itself, apart from action and from objects. Such a consciousness presents in fact the spectacle of mind deprived of its normal functioning, because it is baffled by the actualities in connection with which alone it is truly mind, and is driven back into secluded and impotent revery.

There can be no public without full publicity in respect to all consequences which concern it. Whatever obstructs and restricts publicity, limits and distorts public opinion and checks and distorts thinking on social affairs. Without freedom of expression, not even methods of social inquiry can be developed. For tools can be evolved and perfected only in operation; in application to observing, reporting and organizing actual subject-matter; and this application cannot occur save through free and systematic communication. The early history of physical knowledge, of Greek conceptions of natural phenomena, proves how inept become the conceptions of the best endowed minds when those ideas are elaborated apart from the closest contact with the events which they purport to state and explain. The ruling ideas and methods of the human sciences are in much the same condition to-day. They are also evolved on the basis of past gross observations, remote from constant use in regulation of the material of new observations.

The belief that thought and its communication are now free simply because legal restrictions which once obtained have been done away with is absurd. Its currency perpetuates the infantile state of social knowledge. For it blurs recognition of our central need to possess conceptions which are used as tools of directed inquiry and which are tested, rectified and caused to grow in actual use. No man and no mind was ever emancipated merely by being left alone. Removal of formal limitations is but a negative condition; positive freedom is not a state but an act which involves methods and instrumentalities for control of conditions. Experience shows that sometimes the sense of external oppression, as by censorship, acts as a challenge and arouses intellectual energy and excites courage. But a belief in intellectual freedom where it does not exist contributes only to complacency in virtual enslavement, to sloppiness, superficiality and recourse to sensations as a substitute for ideas: marked traits of our present estate with respect to social knowledge. On one hand, thinking deprived of its normal course takes refuge in academic specialism, comparable in its way to what is called scholasticism. On the other hand, the physical agencies of publicity which exist in such abundance are utilized in ways which constitute a large part of the present meaning of publicity: advertising, propaganda, invasion of private life, the "featuring" of passing incidents in a way which violates all the moving logic of continuity, and which leaves us with those isolated intrusions and shocks which are the essence of "sensations."

It would be a mistake to identify the conditions which limit free communication and circulation of facts and ideas, and which thereby arrest and pervert social thought or inquiry, merely with overt forces which are obstructive. It is true that those who have ability to manipulate social relations for their own advantage have to be reckoned with. They have an uncanny instinct for detecting whatever intellectual tendencies even remotely threaten to encroach upon their control. They have developed an extraordinary facility in enlisting upon their side the inertia, prejudices and emotional partisanship of the masses by use of a technique which impedes free inquiry and expression. We seem to be approaching a state of government by hired promoters of opinion called publicity agents. But the more serious enemy is deeply concealed in hidden entrenchments.

Emotional habituations and intellectual habitudes on the part of the mass of men create the conditions of which the exploiters of sentiment and opinion only take advantage. Men have got used to an experimental method in physical and technical matters. They are still afraid of it in human concerns. The fear is the more efficacious because like all deep-lying fears it is covered up and disguised by all kinds of rationalizations. One of its commonest forms is a truly religious idealization of, and reverence for, established institutions; for example in our own politics, the Constitution, the Supreme Court, private property, free contract and so on. The words "sacred" and "sanctity" come readily to our lips when such things come under discussion. They testify to the religious aureole which protects the institutions. If "holy" means that which is not to be approached nor touched, save with ceremonial precautions and by specially anointed officials, then such things are holy in contemporary political life. As supernatural matters have progressively been left high and dry upon a secluded beach, the actuality of religious taboos has more and more gathered about secular institutions, especially those connected with the nationalistic state.[2] Psychiatrists have discovered that one of the commonest causes of mental disturbance is an underlying fear of which the subject is not aware, but which leads to withdrawal from reality and to unwillingness to think things through. There is a social pathology which works powerfully against effective inquiry into social institutions and conditions. It manifests itself in a thousand ways; in querulousness, in impotent drifting, in uneasy snatching at distractions, in idealization of the long established, in a facile optimism assumed as a cloak, in riotous glorification of things "as they are," in intimidation of all dissenters—ways which depress and dissipate thought all

[2] The religious character of nationalism has been forcibly brought out by Carleton Hayes, in his "Essays on Nationalism," especially Chap. IV.

the more effectually because they operate with subtle and unconscious pervasiveness.

The backwardness of social knowledge is marked in its division into independent and insulated branches of learning. Anthropology, history, sociology, morals, economics, political science, go their own ways without constant and systematized fruitful interaction. Only in appearance is there a similar division in physical knowledge. There is continuous cross-fertilization between astronomy, physics, chemistry and the biological sciences. Discoveries and improved methods are so recorded and organized that constant exchange and intercommunication take place. The isolation of the humane subjects from one another is connected with their aloofness from physical knowledge. The mind still draws a sharp separation between the world in which man lives and the life of man in and by that world, a cleft reflected in the separation of man himself into a body and a mind, which, it is currently supposed, can be known and dealt with apart. That for the past three centuries energy should have gone chiefly into physical inquiry, beginning with the things most remote from man such as heavenly bodies, was to have been expected. The history of the physical sciences reveals a certain order in which they developed. Mathematical tools had to be employed before a new astronomy could be constructed. Physics advanced when ideas worked out in connection with the solar system were used to describe happenings on the earth. Chemistry waited on the advance of physics; the sciences of living things required the material and methods of physics and chemistry in order to make headway.   Human psychology ceased to be chiefly speculative opinion only when biological and physiological conclusions were available. All this is natural and seemingly inevitable.   Things which had the most outlying and indirect connection with human interests had to be mastered in some degree before inquiries could competently converge upon man himself.

Nevertheless the course of development has left us of this age in a plight.   When we say that a subject of science is technically specialized, or that it is highly "abstract," what we practically mean is that it is not conceived in terms of its bearing upon human life.   All *merely* physical knowledge is technical, couched in a technical vocabulary communicable only to the few. Even physical knowledge which does affect human conduct, which does modify what we do and undergo, is also technical and remote in the degree in which its bearings are not understood and used.   The sunlight, rain, air and soil have always entered in visible ways into human experience; atoms and molecules and cells and most other things with which the sciences are occupied affect us, but not visibly.   Because they enter life and modify experience in imperceptible ways, and their consequences are not realized, speech about them is technical; communication is by means of peculiar symbols. One would think, then, that a fundamental and ever-

operating aim would be to translate knowledge of the
subject-matter of physical conditions into terms which
are generally understood, into signs denoting human
consequences of services and disservices rendered. For
ultimately all consequences which enter human life depend upon physical conditions; they can be understood and mastered only as the latter are taken into
account. One would think, then, that any state of affairs which tends to render the things of the environment unknown and incommunicable by human beings in
terms of their own activities and sufferings would be
deplored as a disaster; that it would be felt to be in-
tolerable, and to be put up with only as far as it is, at
any given time, inevitable.

But the facts are to the contrary. Matter and the
material are words which in the minds of many convey
a note of disparagement. They are taken to be foes
of whatever is of ideal value in life, instead of as conditions of its manifestation and sustained being. In
consequence of this division, they do become in fact
enemies, for whatever is consistently kept apart from
human values depresses thought and renders values
sparse and precarious in fact. There are even some
who regard the materialism and dominance of com-
mercialism of modern life as fruits of undue devotion to
physical science, not seeing that the split between
man and nature, artificially made by a tradition which
originated before there was understanding of the
physical conditions that are the medium of human

activities, is the benumbing factor. The most influential form of the divorce is separation between
pure and applied science. Since "application" signifies
recognized bearing upon human experience and well-
being, honor of what is "pure" and contempt for what
is "applied" has for its outcome a science which is
remote and technical, communicable only to specialists,
and a conduct of human affairs which is haphazard,
biased, unfair in distribution of values. What is applied and employed as the alternative to knowledge in
regulation of society is ignorance, prejudice, class-
interest and accident. Science is converted into
knowledge in its honorable and emphatic sense *only* in
application. Otherwise it is truncated, blind, dis-
torted. When it is then applied, it is in ways which
explain the unfavorable sense so often attached to
"application" and the "utilitarian": namely, use for
pecuniary ends to the profit of a few.

At present, the application of physical science is
rather *to* human concerns than *in* them. That is, it
is external, made in the interests of its consequences
for a possessing and acquisitive class. Application *in*
life would signify that science was absorbed and distributed; that it was the instrumentality of that common understanding and thorough communication which
is the precondition of the existence of a genuine and
effective public. The use of science to regulate industry and trade has gone on steadily. The scientific
revolution of the seventeenth century was the precursor

of the industrial revolution of the eighteenth and nine-
teenth. In consequence, man has suffered the impact
of an enormously enlarged control of physical energies
without any corresponding ability to control himself
and his own affairs. Knowledge divided against itself,
a science to whose incompleteness is added an artificial split, has played its part in generating enslavement of men, women and children in factories in which
they are animated machines to tend inanimate machines.
It has maintained sordid slums, flurried and discon-
tented careers, grinding poverty and luxurious wealth,
brutal exploitation of nature and man in times of
peace and high explosives and noxious gases in times
of war. Man, a child in understanding of himself, has
placed in his hands physical tools of incalculable
power. He plays with them like a child, and whether
they work harm or good is largely a matter of accident.
The instrumentality becomes a master and works
fatally as if possessed of a will of its own—not because it has a will but because man has not.

The glorification of "pure" science under such conditions is a rationalization of an escape; it marks a
construction of an asylum of refuge, a shirking of responsibility. The true purity of knowledge exists not
when it is uncontaminated by contact with use and
service. It is wholly a moral matter, an affair of
honesty, impartiality and generous breadth of intent
in search and communication. The adulteration of
knowledge is due not to its use, but to vested bias and

prejudice, to one-sidedness of outlook, to vanity, to conceit of possession and authority, to contempt or disregard of human concern in its use. Humanity is not, as was once thought, the end for which all things were formed; it is but a slight and feeble thing, perhaps an episodic one, in the vast stretch of the universe. But for man, man is the center of interest and the measure of importance. The magnifying of the physical realm at the cost of man is but an abdication and a flight. To make physical science a rival of human interests is bad enough, for it forms a diversion of energy which can ill be afforded. But the evil does not stop there. The ultimate harm is that the understanding by man of his own affairs and his ability to direct them are sapped at their root when knowledge of nature is disconnected from its human function.

It has been implied throughout that knowledge is communication as well as understanding. I well remember the saying of a man, uneducated from the standpoint of the schools, in speaking of certain matters: "Sometime they will be found out and not only found out, but they will be known." The schools may suppose that a thing is known when it is found out. My old friend was aware that a thing is fully known only when it is published, shared, socially accessible. Record and communication are indispensable to knowledge. Knowledge cooped up in a private consciousness is a myth, and knowledge of social phenomena is peculiarly dependent upon dissemination, for only by distribution can such knowledge be either obtained or tested. A fact of community life which is not spread abroad so as to be a common possession is a contradiction in terms. Dissemination is something other than scattering at large. Seeds are sown, not by virtue of being thrown out at random, but by being so distributed as to take root and have a chance of growth. Communication of the results of social inquiry is the same thing as the formation of public opinion. This marks one of the first ideas framed in the growth of political democracy as it will be one of the last to be fulfilled. For public opinion is judgment which is formed and entertained by those who constitute the public and is about public affairs. Each of the two phases imposes for its realization conditions hard to meet.

Opinions and beliefs concerning the public presuppose effective and organized inquiry. Unless there are methods for detecting the energies which are at work and tracing them through an intricate network of interactions to their consequences, what passes as public opinion will be "opinion" in its derogatory sense rather than truly public, no matter how widespread the opinion is. The number who share error as to fact and who partake of a false belief measures power for harm. Opinion casually formed and formed under the direction of those who have something at stake in having a lie believed can be *public* opinion only in name. Calling it by this name, acceptance of the name as a

kind of warrant, magnifies its capacity to lead action
estray. The more who share it, the more injurious its
influence. Public opinion, even if it happens to be cor-
rect, is intermittent when it is not the product of
methods of investigation and reporting constantly at
work. It appears only in crises. Hence its "right-
ness" concerns only an immediate emergency. Its lack
of continuity makes it wrong from the standpoint of
the course of events. It is as if a physician were able
to deal for the moment with an emergency in disease
but could not adapt his treatment of it to the underlying conditions which brought it about. He may then
"cure" the disease—that is, cause its present alarming
symptoms to subside—but he does not modify its
causes; his treatment may even affect them for the
worse. Only continuous inquiry, continuous in the sense
of being connected as well as persistent, can provide the
material of enduring opinion about public matters.

There is a sense in which "opinion" rather than
knowledge, even under the most favorable circumstances, is the proper term to use—namely, in the
sense of judgment, estimate. For in its strict sense,
knowledge can refer only to what *has* happened and
been done. What is still *to be* done involves a forecast
of a future still contingent, and cannot escape the
liability to error in judgment involved in all anticipa-
tion of probabilities. There may well be honest
divergence as to policies to be pursued, even when plans
spring from knowledge of the same facts. But gen-

uinely public policy cannot be generated unless it be informed by knowledge, and this knowledge does not exist except when there is systematic, thorough, and well-equipped search and record.

Moreover, inquiry must be as nearly contemporaneous as possible; otherwise it is only of antiquarian interest. Knowledge of history is evidently necessary for connectedness of knowledge. But history which is not brought down close to the actual scene of events leaves a gap and exercises influence upon the formation of judgments about the public interest only by guess-work about intervening events. Here, only too conspicuously, is a limitation of the existing social sciences. Their material comes too late, too far after the event, to enter effectively into the formation of public opinion about the immediate public concern and what is to be done about it.

A glance at the situation shows that the physical and external means of collecting information in regard to what is happening in the world have far outrun the intellectual phase of inquiry and organization of its results. Telegraph, telephone, and now the radio, cheap and quick mails, the printing press, capable of swift reduplication of material at low cost, have attained a remarkable development. But when we ask what sort of material is recorded and how it is organized, when we ask about the intellectual form in which the material is presented, the tale to be told is very different. "News" signifies something which has just happened, and which is new just because it deviates from the old and regular. But its *meaning* depends upon relation to what it imports, to what its social consequences are. This import cannot be determined unless the new is placed in relation to the old, to what has happened and been integrated into the course of events. Without coördination and consecutiveness, events are not events, but mere occurrences, intrusions; an event implies that out of which a happening proceeds. Hence even if we discount the influence of private interests in procuring suppression, secrecy and misrepresentation, we have here an explanation of the triviality and "sensational" quality of so much of what passes as news. The catastrophic, namely, crime, accident, family rows, personal clashes and conflicts, are the most obvious forms of breaches of continuity; they supply the element of shock which is the strictest meaning of sensation; they are the *new* par excellence, even though only the date of the newspaper could inform us whether they happened last year or this, so completely are they isolated from their connections.

So accustomed are we to this method of collecting, recording and presenting social changes, that it may well sound ridiculous to say that a genuine social science would manifest its reality in the daily press, while learned books and articles supply and polish tools of inquiry. But the inquiry which alone can furnish knowledge as a precondition of public judgments must be contemporary and quotidian. Even if social sciences as a specialized apparatus of inquiry were more advanced than they are, they would be comparatively impotent in the office of directing opinion on matters of concern to the public as long as they are remote from application in the daily and unremitting assembly and interpretation of "news." On the other hand, the tools of social inquiry will be clumsy as long as they are forged in places and under conditions remote from contemporary events.

What has been said about the formation of ideas and judgments concerning the public apply as well to the distribution of the knowledge which makes it an effective possession of the members of the public. Any separation between the two sides of the problem is artificial. The discussion of propaganda and propagandism would alone, however, demand a volume, and could be written only by one much more experienced than the present writer. Propaganda can accordingly only be mentioned, with the remark that the present situation is one unprecedented in history. The political forms of democracy and quasi-democratic habits of thought on social matters have compelled a certain amount of public discussion and at least the simulation of general consultation in arriving at political decisions. Representative government must at least seem to be founded on public interests as they are revealed to public belief. The days are past when government can be carried on without any pretense of ascertaining the wishes of the governed. In

theory, their assent must be secured. Under the older
forms, there was no need to muddy the sources of
opinion on political matters. No current of energy
flowed from them. To-day the judgments popularly
formed on political matters are so important, in spite
of all factors to the contrary, that there is an enormous
premium upon all methods which affect their formation.

The smoothest road to control of political conduct is
by control of opinion. As long as interests of pecuniary profit are powerful, and a public has not located
and identified itself, those who have this interest will
have an unresisted motive for tampering with the
springs of political action in all that affects them. Just
as in the conduct of industry and exchange generally
the technological factor is obscured, deflected and
defeated by "business," so specifically in the management of publicity. The gathering and sale of subject-
matter having a public import is part of the existing
pecuniary system. Just as industry conducted by engineers on a factual technological basis would be a
very different thing from what it actually is, so the
assembling and reporting of news would be a very different thing if the genuine interests of reporters were
permitted to work freely.

One aspect of the matter concerns particularly the
side of dissemination. It is often said, and with a
great appearance of truth, that the freeing and perfecting of inquiry would not have any especial effect.
For, it is argued, the mass of the reading public is not

interested in learning and assimilating the results of accurate investigation. Unless these are read, they cannot seriously affect the thought and action of members of the public; they remain in secluded library alcoves, and are studied and understood only by a few intellectuals. The objection is well taken save as the potency of art is taken into account. A technical high-brow presentation would appeal only to those technically high-brow; it would not be news to the masses. Presentation is fundamentally important, and presentation is a question of art. A newspaper which was only a daily edition of a quarterly journal of sociology or political science would undoubtedly possess a limited circulation and a narrow influence. Even at that, however, the mere existence and accessibility of such material would have some regulative effect. But we can look much further than that. The material would have such an enormous and widespread human bearing that its bare existence would be an irresistible invitation to a presentation of it which would have a direct popular appeal. The freeing of the artist in literary presentation, in other words, is as much a precondition of the desirable creation of adequate opinion on public matters as is the freeing of social inquiry. Men's conscious life of opinion and judgment often proceeds on a superficial and trivial plane. But their lives reach a deeper level. The function of art has always been to break through the crust of conventionalized and routine consciousness. Common things, a flower, a gleam of moonlight, the song of a bird, not things rare and remote, are means with which the deeper levels of life are touched so that they spring up as desire and thought. This process is art. Poetry, the drama, the novel, are proofs that the problem of presentation is not insoluble. Artists have always been the real purveyors of news, for it is not the outward happening in itself which is new, but the kindling by it of emotion, perception and appreciation.

We have but touched lightly and in passing upon the conditions which must be fulfilled if the Great Society is to become a Great Community; a society in which the ever-expanding and intricately ramifying consequences of associated activities shall be known in the full sense of that word, so that an organized, articulate Public comes into being. The highest and most difficult kind of inquiry and a subtle, delicate, vivid and responsive art of communication must take possession of the physical machinery of transmission and circulation and breathe life into it. When the machine age has thus perfected its machinery it will be a means of life and not its despotic master. Democracy will come into its own, for democracy is a name for a life of free and enriching communion. It had its seer in Walt Whitman. It will have its consummation when free social inquiry is indissolubly wedded to the art of full and moving communication.

CHAPTER VI

THE PROBLEM OF METHOD

Perhaps to most, probably to many, the conclusions which have been stated as to the conditions upon which depends the emergence of the Public from its eclipse will seem close to denial of the possibility of realizing the idea of a democratic public. One might indeed point for what it is worth to the enormous obstacles with which the rise of a science of physical things was confronted a few short centuries ago, as evidence that hope need not be wholly desperate nor faith wholly blind. But we are not concerned with prophecy but with analysis. It is enough for present purposes if the problem has been clarified:—if we have seen that the outstanding problem of the Public is discovery and identification of itself, and if we have succeeded, in however groping a manner, in apprehending the conditions upon which the resolution of the problem depends. We shall conclude with suggesting some implications and corollaries as to method, not, indeed, as to the method of resolution, but, once more, the intellectual antecedents of such a method.

The preliminary to fruitful discussion of social matters is that certain obstacles shall be overcome, obstacles residing in our present conceptions of the

185

method of social inquiry. One of the obstructions in the path is the seemingly engrained notion that the first and the last problem which must be solved is the relation of the individual and the social:—or that the outstanding question is to determine the relative merits of individualism and collective or of some compromise between them. In fact, both words, individual and social, are hopelessly ambiguous, and the ambiguity will never cease as long as we think in terms of an antithesis.

In its approximate sense, anything is individual which moves and acts as a unitary thing. For common sense, a certain spatial separateness is the mark of this individuality. A thing is one when it stands, lies or moves as a unit independently of other things, whether it be a stone, tree, molecule or drop of water, or a human being. But even vulgar common sense at once introduces certain qualifications. The tree stands only when rooted in the soil; it lives or dies in the mode of its connections with sunlight, air and water. Then too the tree is a collection of interacting parts; is the tree more a single whole than its cells? A stone moves, apparently alone. But it is moved by something else and the course of its flight is dependent not only upon initial propulsion but upon wind and gravity. A hammer falls, and what was one stone becomes a heap of dusty particles. A chemist operates with one of the grains of dust, and forthwith it disappears in molecules, atoms and electrons—and then? Have we now reached a lonely, but not lonesome, individual? Or does, perhaps, an electron depend for its single and unitary mode of action upon its connections, as much as the stone with which we started? Is its action also a function of some more inclusive and interacting scene?

From another point of view, we have to qualify our approximate notion of an individual as being that which acts and moves as a unitary thing. We have to consider not only its connections and ties, but the consequences with respect to which it acts and moves. We are compelled to say that for some purposes, for some results, the tree is the individual, for others the cell, and for a third, the forest or the landscape. Is a book or a leaf or a folio or a paragraph, or a printer's em *the* individual? Is the binding or the contained thought that which gives individual unity to a book? Or are all of these things definers of an individual according to the consequences which are relevant in a particular situation? Unless we betake ourselves to the stock resort of common sense, dismissing *all* questions as useless quibbles, it seems as if we could not determine an individual without reference to differences made as well as to antecedent and contemporary connections. If so, an individual, whatever else it is or is not, is not just the spatially isolated thing our imagination inclines to take it to be.

Such a discussion does not proceed upon a particularly high nor an especially deep level. But it may at least render us wary of any definition of an individual which operates in terms of separateness. A *distinctive* way of behaving in conjunction and *connection* with other distinctive ways of acting, not a self-enclosed way of acting, independent of everything else, is that toward which we are pointed. Any human being is in one respect an association, consisting of a multitude of cells each living its own life. And as the activity of each cell is conditioned and directed by those with which it interacts, so the human being whom we fasten upon as individual *par excellence* is moved and regulated by his associations with others; what he does and what the consequences of his behavior are, what his experience consists of, cannot even be described, much less accounted for, in isolation.

But while associated behavior is, as we have already noted, a universal law, the fact of association does not of itself make a society. This demands, as we have also seen, perception of the consequences of a joint activity and of the distinctive share of each element in producing it. Such perception creates a common interest; that is concern on the part of each in the joint action and in the contribution of each of its members to it. Then there exists something truly social and not merely associative. But it is absurd to suppose that a society does away with the traits of its own constituents so that it can be set over against them. It can only be set over against the traits which they and their like present in some *other* combination. A molecule of

oxygen in water may act in certain respects differently
than it would in some other chemical union. But *as* a
constituent of water it acts as water does as long as
water is water. The only intelligible distinction which
can be drawn is between the behaviors of oxygen in *its*
different relations, and between those of water in *its*
relations to various conditions, not between that of
water and the oxygen which is conjoined with hydrogen
in water.

A single man when he is joined in marriage is different in that connection to what he was as single or
to what he is in some other union, as a member, say, of
a club. He has new powers and immunities, new responsibilities. He can be contrasted with *himself* as he
behaves in other connections. He may be compared and
contrasted with his wife in their distinctive rôles within
the union. But *as* a member of the union he cannot be
treated as antithetical to the union in which he belongs.
As a member of the union, his traits and acts are evidently those which he possesses in virtue of it, while
those of the integrated association are what they are
in virtue of his status in the union. The only reason
we fail to see this, or are confused by the statement of
it, is because we pass so easily from the man in one connection to the man in some other connection, to the
man not as husband but as business man, scientific in-
vestigator, church-member or citizen, in which connections his acts and their consequences are obviously
different to those due to union in wedlock.

A good example of the fact and of the current confusion as to its interpretation is found in the case of
associations known as limited liability joint-stock com-
panies. A corporation as such is an integrated collective mode of action having powers, rights, duties and
immunities different from those of its singular members
in their other connections. Its different constituents
have also diverse statuses—for example, the owners
of stock from the officers and directors in certain matters. If we do not bear the facts steadily in mind, it
is easy—as frequently happens—to create an artificial
problem. Since the corporation can do things which
its individual members, *in their many relationships outside of their connections in the corporation,* cannot do,
the problem is raised as to the relation of the corporate
collective union to that of individuals *as such.* It is
forgotten that as members of the corporation the individuals themselves are different, have different characteristics, rights and duties, than they would possess
if they were not its members and different from those
which they possess in other forms of conjoint behavior.
But what the individuals may do legitimately *as* members of the corporation in their respective corporate
rôles, the corporation does, and vice versa. A collective
unity may be taken *either* distributively *or* collectively,
but when taken collectively it is the union of its distributive constituents, and when taken distributively,
it is a distribution of and within the collectivity. It
makes nonsense to set up an antithesis between the dis-

tributive phase and the collective. An individual cannot be opposed to the association of which he is an integral part nor can the association be set against its integrated members.

But groups may be opposed to one another, and individuals may be opposed to one another; and an individual as a member of different groups may be divided within himself, and in a true sense have conflicting selves, or be a relatively disintegrated individual. A man may be one thing as a church member and another thing as a member of the business community. The difference may be carried as if in water-tight compartments, or it may become such a division as to entail internal conflict. In these facts we have the ground of the common antithesis set up between society and the individual. Then "society" becomes an unreal abstraction and "*the* individual" an equally unreal one. Because *an* individual can be disassociated from this, that and the other grouping, since he need not be married, or be a church-member or a voter, or belong to a club or scientific organization, there grows up in the mind an image of a residual individual who is not a member of any association at all. From this premise, and from this only, there develops the unreal question of how individuals come to be united in societies and groups: *the* individual and *the* social are now opposed to each other, and there is the problem of "reconciling" them. Meanwhile, the genuine problem is that of adjusting groups and individuals to one another.

The unreal problem becomes particularly acute, as we have already noted in another connection, in times of rapid social change, as when a newly forming industrial grouping with its special needs and energies finds itself in conflict with old established political institutions and their demands. Then it is likely to be forgotten that the actual problem is one of reconstruction of the ways and forms in which men unite in associated activity. The scene presents itself as the struggle of the individual as such to liberate himself from society as such and to claim his inherent or "natural" self-possessed and self-sufficing rights. When the new mode of economic association has grown strong and exercises an overweening and oppressive power over other groupings, the old fallacy persists. The problem is now conceived as that of bringing individuals as such under the control of society as a collectivity. It should still be put as a problem of readjusting social relationships; or, from the distributive side, as that of securing a more equable liberation of the powers of all individual members of all groupings.

Thus our excursion has brought us back to the theme of method, in the interest of which the excursion was taken. One reason for the comparative sterility of discussion of social matters is because so much intellectual energy has gone into the supposititious problem of the relations of individualism and collectivism at large, wholesale, and because the image of the antithesis infects so many specific questions. Thereby thought is

diverted from the only fruitful questions, those of investigation into factual subject-matter, and becomes a
discussion of concepts. The "problem" of the relation
of the concept of authority to that of freedom, of personal rights to social obligations, with only a sub-
sumptive illustrative reference to empirical facts, has
been substituted for inquiry into the *consequences* of
some particular distribution, under given conditions, of
specific freedoms and authorities, and for inquiry into
what altered distribution would yield more desirable
consequences.

As we saw in our early consideration of the theme of
the public, the question of what transactions should be
left as far as possible to voluntary initiative and
agreement and what should come under the regulation
of the public is a question of time, place and concrete
conditions that can be known only by careful observation and reflective investigation. For it concerns consequences; and the nature of consequences and the
ability to perceive and act upon them varies with the
industrial and intellectual agencies which operate. A
solution, or distributive adjustment, needed at one
time is totally unfitted to another situation. That
social "evolution" has been either from collectivism to
individualism or the reverse is sheer superstition. It
has consisted in a continuous re-distribution of social
integrations on the one hand and of capacities and energies of individuals on the other. Individuals find
themselves cramped and depressed by absorption of

their potentialities in some mode of association which
has been institutionalized and become dominant. They
may think they are clamoring for a purely personal
liberty, but what they are doing is to bring into being
a greater liberty to share in other associations, so that
more of their individual potentialities will be released
and their personal experience enriched. Life has been
impoverished, not by a predominance of "society" in
general over individuality, but by a domination of one
form of association, the family, clan, church, economic
institutions, over other actual and possible forms. On
the other hand, the problem of exercising "social control" over individuals is in its reality that of regulating the doings and results of some individuals in order
that a larger number of individuals may have a fuller
and deeper experience. Since both ends can be intelligently attained only by knowledge of actual conditions in their modes of operation and their consequences, it may be confidently asserted that the chief
enemy of a social thinking which would count in public
affairs is the sterile and impotent, because totally irrelevant, channels in which so much intellectual energy
has been expended.

The second point with respect to method is closely
related. Political theories have shared in the absolutistic character of philosophy generally. By this is
meant something much more than philosophies of the
Absolute. Even professedly empirical philosophies have
assumed a certain finality and foreverness in their

theories which may be expressed by saying that they have been non-historical in character. They have isolated their subject-matter from its connections, and any isolated subject-matter becomes unqualified in the degree of its disconnection. In social theory dealing with human nature, a certain fixed and standardized "individual" has been postulated, from whose assumed traits social phenomena could be deduced. Thus Mill says in his discussion of the logic of the moral and social sciences: "The laws of the phenomena of society are, and can be, nothing but the laws of the actions and passions of human beings united together in the social state. Men, however, in a state of society are still men; their actions and passions are obedient to the laws of *individual* human nature." [1] Obviously what is ignored in such a statement is that "the actions and passions" of individual men are in the concrete what they are, their beliefs and purposes included, because of the social medium in which they live; that they are influenced throughout by contemporary and transmitted culture, whether in conformity or protest. What is generic and the same everywhere is at best the organic structure of man, his biological make-up. While it is evidently important to take this into account, it is also evident that none of the *distinctive* features of *human* association can be deduced from it. Thus, in spite of Mill's horror of the metaphysical absolute, his leading social conceptions were, logically, absolutistic. Cer-

[1] J. S. Mill, Logic, Book VI, ch. 7, sec. 1. Italics mine.

tain social laws, normative and regulative, at all periods and under all circumstances of proper social life were assumed to exist.

The doctrine of evolution modified this idea of method only superficially. For "evolution" was itself often understood non-historically. That is, it was assumed that there is a predestined course of fixed stages through which social development must proceed. Under the influence of concepts borrowed from the physical science of the time, it was taken for granted that the very possibility of a social science stood or fell with the determination of fixed uniformities. Now every such logic is fatal to free experimental social inquiry. Investigation into empirical facts was undertaken, of course, but its results had to fit into certain ready-made and second-hand rubrics. When even *physical* facts and laws are perceived and used, social change takes place. The phenomena and laws are not altered, but invention based upon them modifies the human situation. For there is at once an effort to regulate their impact in life. The discovery of malaria does not alter its existential causation, intellectually viewed, but it does finally alter the facts from which the production of malaria arises, through draining and oiling swamps, etc., and by taking other measures of precaution. If the laws of economic cycles of expansion and depression were understood, means would at once be searched for to mitigate if not to do away with the swing. When men have an idea of how social agencies

work and their consequences are wrought, they at
once strive to secure consequences as far as desirable and to avert them if undesirable. These are
facts of the most ordinary observation. But it is not
often noted how fatal they are to the identification of
social with physical uniformities. "Laws" of social
life, when it is genuinely human, are like laws of
engineering. If you want certain results, certain
means must be found and employed. The key to the
situation is a clear conception of consequences wanted,
and of the technique for reaching them, together with,
of course, the state of desires and aversions which
causes some consequences to be wanted rather than
others. All of these things are functions of the preva-
lent culture of the period.

While the backwardness of social knowledge and art
is of course connected with retarded knowledge of
human nature, or psychology, it is also absurd to suppose that an adequate psychological science would
flower in a control of human activities similar to the
control which physical science has procured of physical
energies. For increased knowledge of human nature
would directly and in unpredictable ways modify the
workings of human nature, and lead to the need of new
methods of regulation, and so on without end. It is
a matter of analysis rather than of prophecy to say
that the primary and chief effect of a better psychology would be found in education. The growth and diseases of grains and hogs are now recognized as proper

subjects of governmental subsidy and attention. Instrumental agencies for a similar investigation of the conditions which make for the physical and moral hygiene of the young are in a state of infancy. We spend large sums of money for school buildings and their physical equipment. But systematic expenditure of public funds for scientific inquiry into the conditions which affect the mental and moral development of children is just beginning, and demands for a large increase in this direction are looked upon askance.

Again, it is reported that there are more beds in hospitals and asylums for cases of mental disturbance and retardation than for all diseases combined. The public pays generously to take care of the results of bad conditions. But there is no comparable attention and willingness to expend funds to investigate the causes of these troubles. The reason for these anomalies is evident enough. There is no conviction that the sciences of human nature are far enough advanced to make public support of such activities worth while. A marked development of psychology and kindred subjects would change this situation. And we have been speaking only of antecedent conditions of education. To complete the picture we have to realize the difference which would be made in the methods of parents and teachers were there an adequate and generally shared knowledge of human nature.

But such an educational development, though intrinsically precious to the last degree, would not entail a control of human energies comparable to that which already obtains of physical energies. To imagine that it would is simply to reduce human beings to the plane of inanimate things mechanically manipulated from without; it makes human education something like the training of fleas, dogs and horses. What stands in the way is not anything called "free-will," but the fact that such a change in educational methods would release new potentialities, capable of all kinds of permutations and combinations, which would then modify social phenomena, while this modification would in its turn affect human nature and its educative transformation in a continuous and endless procession.

The assimilation of human science to physical science represents, in other words, only another form of absolutistic logic, a kind of physical absolutism. We are doubtless but at the beginning of the possibilities of control of the physical conditions of mental and moral life. Physiological chemistry, increased knowledge of the nervous system, of the processes and functions of glandular secretions, may in time enable us to deal with phenomena of emotional and intellectual disturbance before which mankind has been helpless. But control of these conditions will not determine the uses to which human beings will put their normalized potentialities. If any one supposes that it will, let him consider the applications of such remedial or preventive measures to a man in a state of savage culture and one in a modern community. Each, as long as the condi-

tions of the social medium remained substantially un-
altered, will still have his experience and the direction of his restored energies affected by the objects
and instrumentalities of the human environment, and
by what men at the time currently prize and hold
dear. The warrior and merchant would be better warriors and merchants, more efficient, but warriors and
merchants still.

These considerations suggest a brief discussion of
the effect of the present absolutistic logic upon the
method and aims of education, not just in the sense
of schooling but with respect to all the ways in which
communities attempt to shape the disposition and beliefs of their members. Even when the processes of
education do not aim at the unchanged perpetuation
of existing institutions, it is assumed that there must
be a mental picture of some desired end, personal and
social, which is to be attained, and that this conception
of a fixed determinate end ought to control educative
processes. Reformers share this conviction with conservatives. The disciples of Lenin and Mussolini vie
with the captains of capitalistic society in endeavoring
to bring about a formation of dispositions and ideas
which will conduce to a preconceived goal. If there
is a difference, it is that the former proceed more
consciously. An experimental social method would
probably manifest itself first of all in surrender of
this notion. Every care would be taken to surround
the young with the physical and social conditions which

best conduce, as far as freed knowledge extends, to release of personal potentialities. The habits thus formed would have entrusted to them the meeting of future social requirements and the development of the future state of society. Then and then only would all social agencies that are available operate as resources in behalf of a bettered community life.

What we have termed the absolutistic logic ends, as far as method in social matters is concerned, in a substitution of discussion of concepts and their logical relations to one another for inquiry. Whatever form it assumes, it results in strengthening the reign of dogma. Their contents may vary, but dogma persists. At the outset we noted in discussion of the state the influence of methods which look for causal forces. Long ago, physical science abandoned this method and took up that of detection of correlation of events. Our language and our thinking is still saturated with the idea of laws which phenomena "obey." But in his actual procedures, the scientific inquirer into physical events treats a law simply as a stable correlation of changes in what happens, a statement of the way in which one phenomenon, or some aspect or phase of it, varies when some other specified phenomenon varies. "Causation" is an affair of historical sequence, of the order in which a series of changes takes place. To know cause and effect is to know, in the abstract, the formula of correlation in change, and, in the concrete, a certain historical career of sequential events. The appeal to causal forces at large not only misleads inquiry into social facts, but it affects equally seriously the formation of purposes and policies.   The person who holds the doctrine of "individualism" or "collectivism" has his program determined for him in advance. It is not with him a matter of finding out the particular thing which needs to be done and the best way, under the circumstances, of doing it.   It is an affair of applying a hard and fast doctrine which follows logically from his preconception of the nature of ultimate causes.   He is exempt from the responsibility of discovering the concrete correlation of changes, from the need of tracing particular sequences or histories of events through their complicated careers.   He knows in advance the sort of thing which must be done, just as in ancient physical philosophy the thinker knew in advance what must happen, so that all he had to do was to supply a logical framework of definitions and classifications.

When we say that thinking and beliefs should be experimental, not absolutistic, we have then in mind a certain logic of method, not, primarily, the carrying on of experimentation like that of laboratories.   Such a logic involves the following factors: First, that those concepts, general principles, theories and dialectical developments which are indispensable to any systematic knowledge be shaped and tested as tools of inquiry. Secondly, that policies and proposals for social action be treated as working hypotheses, not as programs to be rigidly adhered to and executed. They will be experimental in the sense that they will be entertained subject to constant and well-equipped observation of the consequences they entail when acted upon, and subject to ready and flexible revision in the light of observed consequences. The social sciences, if these two stipulations are fulfilled, will then be an apparatus for conducting investigation, and for recording and interpreting (organizing) its results. The apparatus will no longer be taken to be itself knowledge, but will be seen to be intellectual means of making discoveries of phenomena having social import and understanding their meaning. Differences of opinion in the sense of differences of judgment as to the course which it is best to follow, the policy which it is best to try out, will still exist. But opinion in the sense of beliefs formed and held in the absence of evidence will be reduced in quantity and importance. No longer will views generated in view of special situations be frozen into absolute standards and masquerade as eternal truths.

This phase of the discussion may be concluded by consideration of the relation of experts to a democratic public. A negative phase of the earlier argument for political democracy has largely lost its force. For it was based upon hostility to dynastic and oligarchic aristocracies, and these have largely been reft. of power. The oligarchy which now dominates is that of an economic class. It claims to rule, not in virtue of

birth and hereditary status, but in virtue of ability in
management and of the burden of social responsibilities which it carries, in virtue of the position which
superior abilities have conferred upon it.   At all
events, it is a shifting, unstable oligarchy, rapidly
changing its constituents, who are more or less at the
mercy of accidents they cannot control and of technological inventions. Consequently, the shoe is now on
the other foot. It is argued that the check upon the
oppressive power of this particular oligarchy lies in
an intellectual aristocracy, not in appeal to an ignorant, fickle mass whose interests are superficial and
trivial, and whose judgments are saved from incredible
levity only when weighted down by heavy prejudice.

It may be argued that the democratic movement was
essentially transitional. It marked the passage from
feudal institutions to industrialism, and was coincident
with the transfer of power from landed proprietors,
allied to churchly authorities, to captains of industry,
under conditions which involved an emancipation of the
masses from legal limitations which had previously
hemmed them in. But, so it is contended in effect, it is
absurd to convert this legal liberation into a dogma
which alleges that release from old oppressions confers
upon those emancipated the intellectual and moral
qualities which fit them for sharing in regulation of
affairs of state. The essential fallacy of the democratic creed, it is urged, is the notion that a historic
movement which effected an important and desirable

release from restrictions is either a source or a proof
of capacity in those thus emancipated to rule, when in
fact there is no factor common in the two things. The
obvious alternative is rule by those intellectually quali-
fied, by expert intellectuals.

This revival of the Platonic notion that philosophers
should be kings is the more taking because the idea of
experts is substituted for that of philosophers, since
philosophy has become something of a joke, while the
image of the specialist, the expert in operation, is
rendered familiar and congenial by the rise of the
physical sciences and by the conduct of industry. A
cynic might indeed say that the notion is a pipe-dream,
a revery entertained by the intellectual class in com-
pensation for an impotence consequent upon the
divorce of theory and practice, upon the remoteness of
specialized science from the affairs of life: the gulf
being bridged not by the intellectuals but by inventors
and engineers hired by captains of industry. One ap-
proaches the truth more nearly when one says that the
argument proves too much for its own cause. If the
masses are as intellectually irredeemable as its premise
implies, they at all events have both too many desires
and too much power to permit rule by experts to obtain. The very ignorance, bias, frivolity, jealousy,
instability, which are alleged to incapacitate them from
share in political affairs, unfit them still more for passive submission to rule by intellectuals. Rule by an
economic class may be disguised from the masses; rule

by experts could not be covered up. It could be made
to work only if the intellectuals became the willing
tools of big economic interests. Otherwise they would
have to ally themselves with the masses, and that implies, once more, a share in government by the latter.

A more serious objection is that expertness is most
readily attained in specialized technical matters, matters of administration and execution which postulate
that general policies are already satisfactorily framed.
It is assumed that the policies of the experts are in the
main both wise and benevolent, that is, framed to conserve the genuine interests of society. The final obstacle in the way of any aristocratic rule is that in the
absence of an articulate voice on the part of the
masses, the best do not and cannot remain the best, the
wise cease to be wise. It is impossible for high-brows
to secure a monopoly of such knowledge as must be used
for the regulation of common affairs. In the degree
in which they become a specialized class, they are shut
off from knowledge of the needs which they are supposed to serve.

The strongest point to be made in behalf of even
such rudimentary political forms as democracy has already attained, popular voting, majority rule and so
on, is that to some extent they involve a consultation
and discussion which uncover social needs and troubles.
This fact is the great asset on the side of the political
ledger. De Tocqueville wrote it down almost a century ago in his survey of the prospects of democracy

in the United States. Accusing a democracy of a
tendency to prefer mediocrity in its elected rulers, and
admitting its exposure to gusts of passion and its
openness to folly, he pointed out in effect that popular
government is educative as other modes of political
regulation are not. It forces a recognition that there
are common interests, even though the recognition of
what they are is confused; and the need it enforces of
discussion and publicity brings about some clarifica-
tion of what they are. The man who wears the shoe
knows best that it pinches and where it pinches, even
if the expert shoemaker is the best judge of how the
trouble is to be remedied. Popular government has at
least created public spirit even if its success in inform-
ing that spirit has not been great.

A class of experts is inevitably so removed from
common interests as to become a class with private interests and private knowledge, which in social matters
is not knowledge at all. The ballot is, as often said,
a substitute for bullets. But what is more significant
is that counting of heads compels prior recourse to
methods of discussion, consultation and persuasion,
while the essence of appeal to force is to cut short
resort to such methods. Majority rule, just as
majority rule, is as foolish as its critics charge it
with being. But it never is *merely* majority rule.
As a practical politician, Samuel J. Tilden, said a long
time ago: "The means by which a majority comes to be
a majority is the more important thing": antecedent de-

bates, modification of views to meet the opinions of minorities, the relative satisfaction given the latter by the fact that it has had a chance and that next time it may be successful in becoming a majority. Think of the meaning of the "problem of minorities" in certain European states, and compare it with the status of minorities in countries having popular government. It is true that all valuable as well as new ideas begin with minorities, perhaps a minority of one. The important consideration is that opportunity be given that idea to spread and to become the possession of the multitude. No government by experts in which the masses do not have the chance to inform the experts as to their needs can be anything but an oligarchy managed in the interests of the few. And the enlightenment must proceed in ways which force the administrative specialists to take account of the needs. The world has suffered more from leaders and authorities than from the masses.

The essential need, in other words, is the improvement of the methods and conditions of debate, discussion and persuasion. That is *the* problem of the public. We have asserted that this improvement depends essentially upon freeing and perfecting the processes of inquiry and of dissemination of their conclusions. Inquiry, indeed, is a work which devolves upon experts. But their expertness is not shown in framing and executing policies, but in discovering and making known the facts upon which the former depend. They are technical experts in the sense that scientific investigators and artists manifest *expertise.* It is not necessary that the many should have the knowledge and skill to carry on the needed investigations; what is required is that they have the ability to judge of the bearing of the knowledge supplied by others upon common concerns.

It is easy to exaggerate the amount of intelligence and ability demanded to render such judgments fitted for their purpose. In the first place, we are likely to form our estimate on the basis of present conditions. But indubitably one great trouble at present is that the data for good judgment are lacking; and no innate faculty of mind can make up for the absence of facts. Until secrecy, prejudice, bias, misrepresentation, and propaganda as well as sheer ignorance are replaced by inquiry and publicity, we have no way of telling how apt for judgment of social policies the existing intelligence of the masses may be. It would certainly go much further than at present. In the second place, *effective* intelligence is not an original, innate endowment. No matter what are the differences in native intelligence (allowing for the moment that intelligence can be native), the actuality of mind is dependent upon the education which social conditions effect. Just as the specialized mind and knowledge of the past is embodied in implements, utensils, devices and technologies which those of a grade of intelligence which could not produce them can now intelligently use, so it will be when currents of public knowledge blow through social affairs.

The level of action fixed by *embodied* intelligence is always the important thing. In savage culture a superior man will be superior to his fellows, but his knowledge and judgment will lag in many matters far behind that of an inferiorly endowed person in an advanced civilization. Capacities are limited by the objects and tools at hand. They are still more dependent upon the prevailing habits of attention and interest which are set by tradition and institutional customs. Meanings run in the channels formed by instrumentalities of which, in the end, language, the vehicle of thought as well as of communication, is the most important. A mechanic can discourse of ohms and amperes as Sir Isaac Newton could not in his day. Many a man who has tinkered with radios can judge of things which Faraday did not dream of. It is aside from the point to say that if Newton and Faraday were now here, the amateur and mechanic would be infants beside them. The retort only brings out the point: the difference made by different objects to think of and by different meanings in circulation. A more intelligent state of social affairs, one more informed with knowledge, more directed by intelligence, would not improve original endowments one whit, but it would raise the level upon which the intelligence of all operates. The height of this level is much more important for judgment of public concerns than are differences in intelligence quotients. As Santayana has said: "Could a better system prevail in our lives a better order would establish itself in our thinking. It has not been for want of keen senses, or personal genius, or a constant order in the outer world, that mankind has fallen back repeatedly into barbarism and superstition. It has been for want of good character, good example, and good government." The notion that intelligence is a personal endowment or personal attainment is the great conceit of the intellectual class, as that of the commercial class is that wealth is something which they personally have wrought and possess.

A point which concerns us in conclusion passes beyond the field of intellectual method, and trenches upon the question of practical re-formation of social conditions. In its deepest and richest sense a community must always remain a matter of face-to-face intercourse. This is why the family and neighborhood, with all their deficiencies, have always been the chief agencies of nurture, the means by which dispositions are stably formed and ideas acquired which laid hold on the roots of character. The Great Community, in the sense of free and full intercommunication, is conceivable. But it can never possess all the qualities which mark a local community. It will do its final work in ordering the relations and enriching the experience of local associations. The invasion and partial destruction of the life of the latter by outside uncontrolled agencies is the immediate source of the

instability, disintegration and restlessness which characterize the present epoch. Evils which are uncriti-
cally and indiscriminately laid at the door of
industrialism and democracy might, with greater
intelligence, be referred to the dislocation and unsettle-
ment of local communities. Vital and thorough attachments are bred only in the intimacy of an intercourse which is of necessity restricted in range.

Is it possible for local communities to be stable
without being static, progressive without being
merely mobile? Can the vast, innumerable and
intricate currents of trans-local associations be so
banked and conducted that they will pour the generous
and abundant meanings of which they are potential
bearers into the smaller intimate unions of human beings living in immediate contact with one another? Is
it possible to restore the reality of the lesser communal
organizations and to penetrate and saturate their
members with a sense of local community life? There
is at present, at least in theory, a movement away from
the principle of territorial organization to that of
"functional," that is to say, occupational, organization. It is true enough that older forms of territorial
association do not satisfy present needs. It is true
that ties formed by sharing in common work, whether
in what is called industry or what are called professions, have now a force which formerly they did not
possess. But these ties can be counted upon for an enduring and stable organization, which at the same time

is flexible and moving, only as they grow out of immediate intercourse and attachment. The theory, as far
as it relies upon associations which are remote and indirect, would if carried into effect soon be confronted
by all the troubles and evils of the present situation in
a transposed form. There is no substitute for the vi-
tality and depth of close and direct intercourse and
attachment.

It is said, and said truly, that for the world's peace
it is necessary that we understand the peoples of foreign lands. How well do we understand, I wonder, our
next door neighbors? It has also been said that if a
man love not his fellow man whom he has seen, he cannot love the God whom he has not seen. The chances
of regard for distant peoples being effective as long as
there is no close neighborhood experience to bring
with it insight and understanding of neighbors do not
seem better. A man who has not been seen in the daily
relations of life may inspire admiration, emulation,
servile subjection, fanatical partisanship, hero worship; but not love and understanding, save as they
radiate from the attachments of a near-by union.
Democracy must begin at home, and its home is the
neighborly community.

It is outside the scope of our discussion to look into
the prospects of the reconstruction of face-to-face
communities. But there is something deep within human nature itself which pulls toward settled relationships. Inertia and the tendency toward stability

belong to emotions and desires as well as to masses and molecules. That happiness which is full of content and peace is found only in enduring ties with others, which reach to such depths that they go below the surface of conscious experience to form its undisturbed foundation. No one knows how much of the frothy excitement of life, of mania for motion, of fretful discontent, of need for artificial stimulation, is the expression of frantic search for something to fill the void caused by the loosening of the bonds which hold persons together in immediate community of experience. If there is anything in human psychology to be counted upon, it may be urged that when man is satiated with restless seeking for the remote which yields no enduring satisfaction, the human spirit will return to seek calm and order within itself. This, we repeat, can be found only in the vital, steady, and deep relationships which are present only in an immediate community.

The psychological tendency can, however, manifest itself only when it is in harmonious conjunction with the objective course of events. Analysis finds itself in troubled waters if it attempts to discover whether the tide of events is turning away from dispersion of energies and acceleration of motion. Physically and externally, conditions have made, of course, for concentration; the development of urban, at the expense of rural, populations; the corporate organization of aggregated wealth, the growth of all sorts of organizations, are evidence enough. But enormous organization is compatible with demolition of the ties that form local communities and with substitution of impersonal bonds for personal unions, with a flux which is hostile to stability. The character of our cities, of organized business and the nature of the comprehensive associations in which individuality is lost, testify also to this fact. Yet there are contrary signs. "Community" and community activities are becoming words to conjure with. The local is the ultimate universal, and as near an absolute as exists. It is easy to point to many signs which indicate that unconscious agencies as well as deliberate planning are making for such an enrichment of the experience of local communities as will conduce to render them genuine centers of the attention, interest and devotion for their constituent members.

The unanswered question is how far these tendencies will reëstablish the void left by the disintegration of the family, church and neighborhood. We cannot predict the outcome. But we can assert with confidence that there is nothing intrinsic in the forces which have effected uniform standardization, mobility and remote invisible relationships that is fatally obstructive to the return movement of their consequences into the local homes of mankind. Uniformity and standardization may provide an underlying basis for differentiation and liberation of individual potentialities. They may sink to the plane of unconscious habituations, taken for

granted in the mechanical phases of life, and deposit a
soil from which personal susceptibilities and endowments
may richly and stably flower. Mobility may in the
end supply the means by which the spoils of remote
and indirect interaction and interdependence flow back
into local life, keeping it flexible, preventing the
stagnancy which has attended stability in the past,
and furnishing it with the elements of a variegated
and many-hued experience. Organization may cease
to be taken as an end in itself. Then it will no longer
be mechanical and external, hampering the free play of
artistic gifts, fettering men and women with chains of
conformity, conducing to abdication of all which does
not fit into the automatic movement of organization as
a self-sufficing thing. Organization as a means to an
end would reënforce individuality and enable it to be
securely itself by enduing it with resources beyond its
unaided reach.

Whatever the future may have in store, one thing is
certain. Unless local communal life can be restored,
the public cannot adequately resolve its most urgent
problem: to find and identify itself. But if it be re-
established, it will manifest a fullness, variety and
freedom of possession and enjoyment of meanings and
goods unknown in the contiguous associations of the
past. For it will be alive and flexible as well as stable,
responsive to the complex and world-wide scene in
which it is enmeshed. While local, it will not be
isolated. Its larger relationships will provide an inex-

haustible and flowing fund of meanings upon which to draw, with assurance that its drafts will be honored. Territorial states and political boundaries will persist; but they will not be barriers which impoverish experience by cutting man off from his fellows; they will not be hard and fast divisions whereby external separation is converted into inner jealousy, fear, suspicion and hostility. Competition will continue, but it will be less rivalry for acquisition of material goods, and more an emulation of local groups to enrich direct experience with appreciatively enjoyed intellectual and artistic wealth. If the technological age can provide mankind with a firm and general basis of material security, it will be absorbed in a humane age. It will take its place as an instrumentality of shared and communicated experience. But without passage through a machine age, mankind's hold upon what is needful as the precondition of a free, flexible and many-colored life is so precarious and inequitable that competitive scramble for acquisition and frenzied use of the results of acquisition for purposes of excitation and display will be perpetuated.

We have said that consideration of this particular condition of the generation of democratic communities and an articulate democratic public carries us beyond the question of intellectual method into that of practical procedure. But the two questions are not disconnected. The problem of securing diffused and seminal intelligence can be solved only in the degree in which local communal life becomes a reality. Signs and symbols, language, are the means of communication by which a fraternally shared experience is ushered in and sustained. But the wingèd words of conversation in immediate intercourse have a vital import lacking in the fixed and frozen words of written speech. Systematic and continuous inquiry into all the conditions which affect association and their dissemination in print is a precondition of the creation of a true public. But it and its results are but tools after all. Their final actuality is accomplished in face-to-face relationships by means of direct give and take. Logic in its fulfillment recurs to the primitive sense of the word: dialogue. Ideas which are not communicated, shared, and reborn in expression are but soliloquy, and soliloquy is but broken and imperfect thought. It, like the acquisition of material wealth, marks a diversion of the wealth created by associated endeavor and exchange to private ends. It is more genteel, and it is called more noble. But there is no difference in kind.

In a word, that expansion and reënforcement of personal understanding and judgment by the cumulative and transmitted intellectual wealth of the community which may render nugatory the indictment of democracy drawn on the basis of the ignorance, bias and levity of the masses, can be fulfilled only in the relations of personal intercourse in the local community. The connections of the ear with vital and out-going thought and emotion are immensely closer and more

varied than those of the eye. Vision is a spectator;
hearing is a participator. Publication is partial and
the public which results is partially informed and
formed until the meanings it purveys pass from mouth
to mouth. There is no limit to the liberal expansion
and confirmation of limited personal intellectual endowment which may proceed from the flow of social
intelligence when that circulates by word of mouth
from one to another in the communications of the local
community. That and that only gives reality to public
opinion. We lie, as Emerson said, in the lap of an
immense intelligence. But that intelligence is dormant
and its communications are broken, inarticulate and
faint until it possesses the local community as its
medium.

AFTERWORD

This book was written some twenty years ago. It is my belief that intervening events confirm the position about the public and its connection with the state as the political organization of human relationships that was then presented. The most obvious consideration is the effect of the Second World War in weakening the conditions to which we give the Name "Isolationism." The First World War had enough of that effect to call the League of Nations into being. But the United States refused to participate. And, while out-and-out nationalism was a prime factor in the refusal, it was reinforced by the strong belief that, after all, the main purpose of the League was to preserve the fruits of victory for the European nations that were on the winning side. There is no need to revive old controversies by discussing how far that belief was justifiable. The important fact for the issue here discussed is that the *belief* that such was the case was a strongly actuating consideration in the refusal of the United States to join the League. After the Second World War, this attitude was so changed that the country joined the United Nations.

What is the bearing of this fact upon the position

taken in the book regarding the public and the connection of the public with the political aspects of social life? In brief, it is as follows: The decline, (though probably not for a rather long future time the obliteration) of Isolationism is evidence that there is developing the sense that relations between nations are taking on the properties that constitute a public, and hence call for some measure of political organization. Just what the measure is to be, how far political authority is to extend, is a question still in dispute. There are those who would hold it to the strictest possible construction of the code for the United Nations adopted at San Francisco. There are others who urge the necessity of altering the code so as to provide for a World Federation having wide political authority.

It is aside from the point here under consideration to discuss which party is right. The very fact that there are two parties, that there is an active dispute, is evidence that the question of the relations between nations which in the past have claimed and exercised singular sovereignty has now definitely entered the arena of political problems. It is pointed out in the text of this book that the scope, the range, of the public, the question of where the public shall end and the sphere of the private begin, has long been a vital political problem in domestic affairs. At last the same issue is actively raised about the relations between national units, no one of which in the past has acknowledged *political* responsibility in the conduct of its policies toward other national units. There has been acknowledgment of *moral* responsibility. But the same thing holds good in relations that are private and nonpolitical; the chief difference is the greater ease with which moral responsibility broke down in the case of relationships between nations. The very doctrine of "Sovereignty" is a complete denial of political responsibility.

The fact that this issue is now within the active scope of political discussion also bears out another point made in the text. The matter at issue is in no way one between the "social" and the "non-social," or between that which is moral and that which is immoral. No doubt the feeling on the part of some that the moral responsibility which concerns the relations between nations should be taken more seriously played a part in bringing about a greater emphasis on the fact that the consequences of these relations demand some kind of political organization. But only the ultra-cynical have ever denied in the past the existence of some moral responsibility. Sufficient proof of this is found in the fact that, in order to interest the citizens of any genuinely modern people in an actual war, it has been necessary to carry on a campaign to show that *superior* moral claims were on the side of a

war policy. The change of attitude is not fundamentally an affair of moral conversion, a change from
obdurate immorality to a perception of the claims of
righteousness. It results from greatly intensified recognition of the factual consequences of war. And this
increased perception is in turn mainly due to the fact
that modern wars are indefinitely more destructive
and that the destruction occurs over a much wider
geographical area than was the case in the past. It is no
longer possible to argue that war brings positive good.
The most that can be said is that it is a choice of the
lesser moral evil.

The fact that the problem of the scope of the political relations between nations has now entered the
arena of political discussion, goes to confirm another
point emphasized in the book. The same problem of
where the line is to be drawn between affairs left to
private consideration and those subject to political
adjudication is *formally* a universal problem. But with
respect to the actual content taken by the problem, the
question is always a *concrete* one. That is, it is a question
of specifying factual consequences, which are never
inherently fixed nor subject to determination in terms
of abstract theory. Like all facts subject to observation
and specification, they are spatial-temporal, not eternal. (*The State* is pure myth. And, as is pointed out in
the text, the very notion of the state as a universal

ideal and norm arose at a particular space-time junc-
ture to serve quite concrete aims.)

Suppose for example that the idea of federation, as
distinct from both isolation and imperial rule, is accepted as a working principle. Some things are settled,
but not the question of just what affairs come within
the jurisdiction of the Federated Government and
which are excluded and remain for decision by national units as such. The problem of what should be
included and what excluded from federated authority
would become acute. And in the degree in which the
decision on this point is made intelligently, it will be
made on the ground of foreseen, concrete consequences likely to result from adopting alternative
policies. And just as in the case of domestic political
affairs, there will be the problem of discovering something of common interest amid the conflict of separate
interests of the distinctive units. Friendship is not the
cause of arrangements that serve the common interests
of several units, but the outcome of the arrangements.
General theory might indeed be helpful; but it would
serve intelligent decision only if it were used as an
aid to foreseeing factual consequences, not directly
per se.

Thus far, (I have kept discussion within what I find
to be the field of facts sufficiently evident so that any
one who so desires can take note of them.) I come now

to a point that trenches actively upon the field of important, unsettled hypotheses. In the second chapter of
the text, changes in "material culture" are mentioned
as an important factor in shaping the concrete conditions which determine the consequences that are of the
kind called "public" and that lead to some sort of
political intervention. If there were ever any reasonable doubt of the import of technological factors with
respect to socially significant human consequences,
that time is well past. Nor is the importance of technological development confined to domestic issues,
great as it is in this field. The enormously increased
destructiveness of war, previously mentioned is the
immediate outcome of modern technological developments. And the frictions and conflicts which are the
immediate occasion of wars are due to the infinitely
multiplied and more intricate points of contact between peoples which in turn are the direct result of
technological developments.

So far we are still within the bounds of the observable facts of the transactions that occur between national units in the same way they occur between the
members of a given domestic unit. The unsettled question that now looms as the irrepressible conflict of the
future pertains to the actual range of the economic
factor in determination of specific consequences. As
will be seen by consulting the index, s.v. "Economic

Forces and Politics," the immense influence exercised
by economic aspects of modern life receives attention.
But as far as concerned political relations between
national units, the question then had to do mainly
with special issues such as tariffs most favored treatment, retaliation, etc. The view that economics is the
sole condition affecting the entire range of political
organization and that present day industry impera-
tively demands a certain single type of social organization has been a *theoretical* issue because of the
influence of the writings of Marx. But, in spite of the
revolution in Soviet Russia, it was hardly an immediate *practical* issue of international politics. Now it is
definitely becoming such an issue, and present signs
point to its being a *predominant* issue in determining the
future of international political relationships.

The position that economics is the sole conditioning
factor of political organization, together with the
position that all phases and aspects of social life, science, art, education and all the agencies of public communication included, are determined by the type of
economy that prevails is identical with that type of
life to which the name "totalitarian" justly applies.
Given the view that there is but one form of economic
organization that properly fulfills social conditions,
and that one country of all the peoples of the earth
has attained that state in an adequate degree, there

is in existence an outstanding and overshadowing practical problem.

For Soviet Russia has now arrived at a state of power and influence in which an intrinsically totalitarian philosophy has passed from the realm of theory into that of the practical political relations of the national states of the globe. The problem of adjusting the relations of states sufficiently democratic to put a considerable measure of trust in free inquiry and open discussion, as a fundamental method in peaceable negotiation of social conflicts, with the point of view that there is but one Truth, fixed and absolute and hence not open to inquiry and public discussion, is now a vital one. Although my own belief as to where the line of social progress is to be drawn between the two positions is firmly in accord with that of the great majority of members of democratic states (I am not here concerned with considerations of right and wrong, of truth or falsity). I cannot refrain, however, from pointing out how the world situation bears out the hypothesis that the matter of the scope or range and of the seriousness of the factual consequences of associated human transactions is the determining factor in affecting social behavior with *political* properties too evident to be ignored. The problem of discovering and implementing politically areas of common interest is henceforth imperative.

There is one other point that demands attention. The text points out in a number of places, firstly, that *noting* of consequences is an indispensable condition over and above their mere occurrence and, secondly, that this noting (on anything like an adequate scale) depends upon the state of knowledge at the time, especially upon the degree to which kind of method called scientific is applied to social affairs. Some of us have been insisting for some time that science bears exactly the same relation to the progress of culture as do the affairs acknowledged to be technological (like the state of invention in the case, say, of tools and machinery, or the progress reached in the arts, say, the medical). We have also held that a considerable part of the remediable evils of present life are due to the state of imbalance of scientific method with respect to its application to physical facts on one side and to specifically human facts on the other side; and that the most direct and effective way out of these evils is steady and systematic effort to develop that effective intelligence named scientific method in the case of human transactions.

Our theorizing on this point cannot be said to have had much effect. The relative importance of the consequences of events which are of the nature of theorizing, and of events which are so overt as to force themselves upon general attention is well exhibited in what has followed upon the fission of the atom. Its consequences are so impressive that there is not only a clamor, approaching a Babel, about the utility and disutility of physical sciences, but some aspects of the control of science in the interest of social well-being have entered the arena of politics,—of governmental discussion and action. In evidence, it is enough to point to the controversy going on in the Congress of the United States as these pages are written as to civilian and military participation in control, and in the United Nations as to the best method in general of managing the needed control.

Aspects of the *moral* problem of the status of physical science have been with us for a long time. But the consequences of the physical sciences, though immeasurably important to industry, and through industry in society generally, failed to obtain the kind of observation that would bring the conduct and state of science into the specifically *political* field. The use of these sciences to increase the destructiveness of war was brought to such a sensationally obvious focus with the splitting of the atom that the political issue is now with us, whether or no.

There are those who not only insist upon taking an exclusively moralistic view of science but who also insist upon doing so in an extremely one-sided way. They put the blame for the present evils on physical science as if it were a causal entity *per se,* and not a human product which does what prevailing human institutions exact of it. They then use the evils that are apparent as a ground for the subjection of science to what they take to be moral ideals and standards, in disregard of the fact, hortatory preaching aside, there is no method of accomplishing this subordination save setting up some institution equipped with absolute authority—the sure way to restore the kind of conflict that once marked the attempt of the Church to control scientific inquiry. The net outcome of their position, were it adopted, would not be the subordination of science to ideal moral aims, in disregard of political or public interests, but the production of political despotism with all the moral evils which attend that mode of social organization.

Science, being a human construction, is as much subject to human use as any other technological development. But, unfortunately, "use" includes misuse and abuse. Holding science to be an entity by itself, as is done in most of the current distinctions between science as "pure" and "applied," and then blaming it for social evils, like those of economic maladjustment and destruction in war, with a view to subordinating it to moral ideals, is of no positive benefit. On the contrary, it distracts us from using our knowledge and our most competent methods of observation in the performance of the work they are able to do. This work is the promotion of effective foresight of the consequences of social policies and institutional arrangements.

John Dewey

Hubbards, Nova Scotia
July 22, 1946

INDEX

233